"I have often wished that I could clone this team for thousands of parents. They arrive in therapy or Christian r⸱   ⸱d about their children coming out. T   d resource that is also full of personal  n-ilies in a personal and relatable wa   ⸱f-ficult to hear, but it offers a realisti   e and Zaporozhets have shared their v   ⸱o have landed in the middle of a culture war. It is a guide to loving their children well in this circumstance."

Jennifer Ripley, Hughes Endowed Chair of Christian Integration at Regent University

"This is the very book I've wished I had on my bookshelf every time a Christian parent reaches out to me after their child comes out to them. In these pages, they hear their own story—what has been, what is, and what might yet unfold—and they see that they are neither alone nor way off mark in walking this journey with their child, with God, and with their church. Yarhouse and Zaporozhets provide grounding, empathy, and hope for parents as well as insight and direction for pastors and churches who want to minister to them."

Janet B. Dean, psychologist and professor of pastoral counselor education at Asbury Theological Seminary

"*When Children Come Out* is an essential read for conservative Christian parents who have discovered their child is LGBTQ+. Mark Yarhouse and Olya Zaporozhets have done an extraordinary job in marrying statistical data with real-life stories. This book lays the framework that helps parents become educated on the topic and provides applications that will bring hope and healing to hurting families. We wish this book had been available to us when we found out our son is gay. This book will indeed save lives."

Greg and Lynn McDonald, cofounders of Embracing the Journey

"This much-needed research is a gift not only to Christian parents of LGBTQ+ kids but also to the communities that love them. In these pages, Christian parents can learn from others with similar experiences and be reminded that they're not alone, and supportive communities can gain insight into the likely milestones of these parents' journeys. As an LGBTQ+ kid who loves my own Christian parents (and many others as well), I'm thrilled to see this book out in the world."

Gregory Coles, author of *Single, Gay Christian* and *No Longer Strangers*

"Yarhouse and Zaporozhets helpfully illumine the complex realities Christian parents face when journeying with their children who identify as LGBTQ+. Drawing from decades of research and the extensive experiences of other parents who have already taken this road, this book offers wise guidance for both Christian parents and churches. In particular, it offers a map of what to expect along the pilgrimage and advice for loving conversations in pursuit of redemptive, Christlike relationships along the way."

Perry Glanzer, professor of educational foundations at Baylor University

WHEN CHILDREN COME OUT

A GUIDE FOR CHRISTIAN PARENTS

MARK YARHOUSE AND OLYA ZAPOROZHETS

Academic

An imprint of InterVarsity Press
Downers Grove, Illinois

InterVarsity Press
P.O. Box 1400 | Downers Grove, IL 60515-1426
ivpress.com | email@ivpress.com

InterVarsity Press® is the publishing division of InterVarsity Christian Fellowship/USA®. For more information, visit intervarsity.org.

All Scripture quotations, unless otherwise indicated, are taken from The Holy Bible, New International Version®, NIV®. Copyright © 1973, 1978, 1984, 2011 by Biblica, Inc.™ Used by permission of Zondervan. All rights reserved worldwide. www.zondervan.com. The "NIV" and "New International Version" are trademarks registered in the United States Patent and Trademark Office by Biblica, Inc.™

While any stories in this book are true, some names and identifying information may have been changed to protect the privacy of individuals.

The publisher cannot verify the accuracy or functionality of website URLs used in this book beyond the date of publication.

Cover design and image composite: David Fassett
Interior design: Jeanna Wiggins

ISBN 978-1-5140-0008-3 (print) | ISBN 978-1-5140-0009-0 (digital)

Printed in the United States of America ♾

Library of Congress Cataloging-in-Publication Data
A catalog record for this book is available from the Library of Congress.

29   28   27   26   25   24   23   22 | 13   12   11   10   9   8   7   6   5   4   3   2   1

CONTENTS

ACKNOWLEDGMENTS

MANY RESEARCHERS HAVE BEEN INVOLVED in the projects we cite throughout this book. We wish to acknowledge in particular the work of Justin Sides, Melissa Campbell, Ashley Allen, Dara Houp, Kathryn Maslowe, and Tiffany Erspamer, who completed dissertations on the experiences of Christian parents. We also want recognize those who assisted with consensual qualitative analysis and other data analysis, including our former colleague, Elisabeth Suarez, as well as former students Julia Sadusky, Joshua Matlack, Heather Keefe, Seth Crocker, Carson Fuhrman, Chelsi Creech, Morgan Nicolas, Emma Bucher, Tranese Morgan, and Shane Ferrell. Students at the Sexual & Gender Identity Institute at Wheaton College who worked on our most recent surveys include Chuck Cruise, Kevin Biondolillo, Micaela Hardyman, Ashley Lewis, Anne Seibert, Ethan Martin, Nicholas Amitrano, and Matthew McRay. Students at the Institute for the Study of Sexual Identity at Regent University who worked on our most recent surveys included Michael Haarer and Alex Newcomer. Our Sexual & Gender Identity Institute Fellows—Stephen Stratton, Janet Dean, and Julia Sadusky—continue to provide countless hours of consultation and feedback on original projects that inform this book through and through. We are also grateful to Greg Coles, who helped copyedit the early draft of this book, as well as to Jon Boyd, our editor at IVP Academic, for his editorial guidance throughout.

WHAT THIS BOOK IS ABOUT AND WHY IT MATTERS, OR WHO WE ARE AND HOW TO READ THIS BOOK

PATIENCE AND LEONARD, parents of a teenage boy, recently sat down across from me at the end of a consultation. Leonard was staring straight ahead, showing little emotion. Patience said she was feeling tired and just overwhelmed by everything. Their son, Matthew, had come out as gay this past year, and they were feeling confused and unsure how to respond. Just before they came to our meeting, their son had said he no longer believed in God.

During the consultation, both parents shared how they responded when Matthew shared with them about his same-sex sexuality. Leonard had not really said anything. He had been quiet. In our meeting today, he shared that his silence was probably interpreted by Matthew as anger or even rejection. He wasn't sure. They hadn't discussed it. Patience had been in tears and just didn't know what to say.

Since that time, they have been going over and over in their minds as many key moments in their parenting as they could recall. Decisions about playdates, clothing, family devotions, summer camp, sleepovers, taking a promotion, moving from one part of the state to another, and so much more—any decision that might provide a clue as to the origins of Matthew's sexual orientation. In our time together we reflected on what it meant to them to identify a cause, to seemingly desire to take responsibility for their son's sexuality so they could at least have an explanation for its existence. "It was me," said Leonard. "I wasn't there as much as I should have been. I know that's what it is."

I (Mark) was able to talk with them about what we know and do not know about the origins of same-sex sexuality or a homosexual orientation, and I listened to their concerns and fears while sharing my own view that I did not think they did anything or failed to do something that caused Matthew to experience same-sex sexuality. I shared with them that they are describing common parenting challenges and decisions but that I wanted to release them from what seemed like an indictment they were making against themselves. They hadn't done anything to make Matthew gay. They hadn't failed to do something that made Matthew gay.

But what we could put our energy toward today was being in a relationship with Matthew so that he would know they loved him and wanted to find ways to be a source of encouragement and support. With the recent news about Matthew's faith, we discussed being in relationship with Matthew where their own authentic faith could motivate them to stay engaged and to model the love that God has for Matthew.

We wrote this book to offer Christian parents a research-informed understanding of what it's like when a child like Matthew comes out. Christian parents don't all share a single story, and we don't mean to imply that they do by writing a book on the subject. Still, as we have listened to many Christian parents sharing from their hearts—and often through their tears—we have learned that these parents encounter many similar experiences. There are regrets, and there is hope. There are challenges, but there are also opportunities. In addition to helping parents be better informed and supported in their journeys, we want this book to help the church be better positioned as a resource to Christian parents navigating difficult terrain.

How is this book organized? We start with the moment of awareness, whether that comes from a child's voluntary disclosure or a more accidental or unwanted discovery. From that point, parents begin to become aware they may need to seek help. They are also trying to find ways to maintain their relationship with their child, which can be strained. We then turn to a discussion of how the relationship with their child changes over time—what worsens initially but tends to get better over time. We then discuss how faith changes over time for Christian parents before covering what it means to come to terms with the reality of their child's disclosure of same-sex sexuality or gender identity. Coming to terms with something happens at several levels of experience. We close the book by turning to the question of how the church could be supportive of Christian parents through this journey.

> *We wrote this book to offer Christian parents a research-informed understanding of what it's like when a child comes out.*

You will see at the end of each chapter two features. One is called "Advice from Christian Parents." This is where we let other Christian parents who have been walking out this journey share from their own experience. They offer pearls of wisdom from their own life that may be especially helpful to you. The other special feature is "Your Turn." This is an opportunity for you to process what you've read and apply it your circumstances. Every story is unique. Your story is unique. We want you to take what you are reading, have an opportunity to digest it, and see whether you can apply it to your circumstances in ways that are helpful to you.

We use the terms *LGBTQ+* (lesbian, gay, bisexual, transgender, queer, and other experiences) and *gay* throughout this book as umbrella terms for a larger constellation of experiences of same-sex sexuality of diverse gender identities. This is the language we saw in our transcribed interviews and the language of the children of the interviewed parents, and it seems fitting to use that language here. Of course, each person uses the language that best fits their experience and attributions about what same-sex sexuality or different gender identities mean to them, and we use excerpts from interviews that capture a range of expressions of identity.

In order to offer a research-informed perspective, we have drawn on the work of several research projects in writing this book. Our largest data source is a qualitative study of over two hundred Christian parents who had a child come out to them as LGBTQ+. This study was conducted by the Marin Foundation in Chicago. Laura Statesir was instrumental in that project. The Institute for the Study of Sexual Identity analyzed the study's data at the request of the Marin Foundation's president, Andrew Marin. That data was presented at several professional conferences, became the basis of nearly half a dozen dissertations, and was even published in peer-reviewed scientific journal articles. We cite these publications, presentations, and dissertations throughout this book. Although the Marin Foundation has since closed its doors, we continue to analyze the data we received from it, and Andrew Marin has given us permission to feature that data here.

In addition to discussing this large study, we also draw from three other data sources. First, we cite a study conducted through the Institute for the Study of Sexual Identity and eventually published in the *American Journal of Family Therapy*.[1] Second, we discuss findings from our quantitative study of 125 Christian parents who had a child come out to them as same-sex attracted, gender diverse, or LGBTQ+.[2] Finally, we cite our study of 229 LGBTQ+ adults who had come out to Christian parents.[3]

Several Christian parents also contributed brief essays on some aspect of their experience of a child coming out to them as LGBTQ+. We want to thank Dave and Jean Coles, Greg and Lynn McDonald, and Barclay Jones (pseudonym) for their willingness to share their thoughts and experiences. Apart from these parents being named, all other names have been changed to protect the identities of family members. In several quotes that used the name of a son or daughter, we have replaced this name with the bracketed words "my son" or "my daughter." Most of the book is geared toward parents of children who are lesbian, gay, bisexual, or queer, but we offer breakout boxes in each chapter on some of the unique aspects of the topic covered in that chapter as it applies to parents of children who come out as transgender.

Both authors of this book have extensive experience working with individuals and families navigating sexual identity, gender identity, and religious faith. Mark Yarhouse is the Dr. Arthur P. Rech & Mrs. Jean May Rech Professor of Psychology at Wheaton College, where he directs the Sexual & Gender Identity Institute. For more than two decades, Mark has conducted research on and provided clinical services to individuals, couples, and families navigating conflicts between their sexual or gender identity and their religious identity.

Olya Zaporozhets is an associate professor in the School of Psychology and Counseling at Regent University. As director of research for the Institute for the Study of Sexual Identity, she has overseen research on the experiences of Christian parents when their children come out to them as LGBTQ+. She is also actively involved with the international research community and edited a Russian edition of *Sexuality and Sex Therapy: A Comprehensive Christian Appraisal* (by Yarhouse and Tan). She has curated the counseling skills education and training of Ukrainian students in response to wartime needs.

Circling back to Patience, Leonard, and Matthew, I could visibly see the weight come off of both Patience and Leonard when they took in this new information—that they had not caused their son, Matthew, to experience same-sex attraction. Over the next few months, they seemed to have renewed energy that they could direct toward their relationship with Matthew. They began praying more about how to model Christ to their son and how to offer a consistent rhythm of daily faith, not that it was ever on display but just as a normal, organic expression of who they were.

These practices seemed to ground them more than create a change in Matthew. They had less fear. They began to ask Matthew better questions or prompts about his experiences, such as, "Tell us how you first became aware of your same-sex sexuality and how you made sense of it at the time." Through coaching they received in counseling, they did not use these prompts to attempt to trick Matthew in any way. They did not critique what Matthew shared, nor did they defend other ways of thinking about his experiences. They listened. They expressed appreciation for what their son was willing to share. They kept as many points of contact open in their relationship, growing in confidence that their relationship would continue even as Matthew had more options to be on his own and outside their immediate influence.

This was not a quick turnaround. This was a slow process, like steering a heavy ship in deep water. By the way, it turned out that Matthew did still believe in God, but he didn't connect with the people who represented God to him in ways that felt rejecting. He had his own journey of faith that he was on, and he was open to sharing more of that with his parents as they rebuilt their relationship with one another.

> *By the way, it turned out that Matthew did still believe in God.*

This book examines the coming-out experience of LGBTQ+ people through the eyes of their Christian parents. However, we are not only concerned in this book with the experiences of those who come out; we also portray the journey that many Christian parents have undertaken with their child as they navigate both the initial coming out and the months and years that follow, as they enter into a new relationship with the child they love.[4] We hope the information here will be of help to parents navigating similar terrain. We also hope that learning the experiences of Christian parents can help the church to offer a more nuanced ministry approach to parents and families in the coming years.

1

HOW PARENTS BECOME AWARE

Dear Mom and Dad,

I want to share something that has been hard for me to talk about with you. Since I first felt romantic feelings for others, which was about the time I went through puberty, I have been attracted more to girls than to boys. This is something I haven't always understood or had any idea what to do about. It isn't something that I chose to feel or that I'm choosing today to feel to upset you or make life more complicated. I've had these feelings for many years, and I have been trying to find a way to share what I've been feeling and thinking with you.

I've also struggled with shame for many years. I finally realized that I don't have to be ashamed of something I didn't choose. I also believe in my heart that God loves me.

You may be wondering about relationships, dating, and all of that. But that is not what this letter is about. To be honest, it's an area that I am continuing to pray about and ask God about.

I know this is very different from what you may have known about growing up, and it may take time to process. I'm open to talking about this with you and answering questions you may have. I am sharing this part of my experience with different people in my life and at my own pace as I feel safe and comfortable. I just wanted to find the words to share this with you too. Our relationship matters to me, and that's why I am taking this step to share more of myself with you. I am still the Lorelei I have always been, and I still love you both very much.

This letter from Lorelei, written when she was twenty-four years old, represents a first step many LGBTQ+ young people make to share more of themselves with their parents.

We understand that not every parent receives a letter as well-worded as this, and we recognize that the nature of a child's initial coming out may very well set the stage for future experiences and dynamics. Also, complicating circumstances can add layers of complexity to the parent-child relationship.

There is no one coming-out experience shared by all parents, not even by all Christian parents. You and your family are on *your* journey.

At the same time, there is much to be gained from hearing the experiences of Christian parents such as Lorelei's. You may benefit from knowing you are not alone and that other Christian parents have had similar experiences or asked similar questions or faced similar challenges. If you are the parent of an LGBTQ+ child—or the parent of a child who might someday disclose to you that they are LGBTQ+— some of the accounts offered in this book may not resonate with you, while others likely will. Even if something doesn't match your experience, you still may benefit from reading how other Christian parents have responded, what their relationships looked like, how they responded to a different set of circumstances, and so on. Regardless, we believe that reading these accounts can help you as you face important decisions and wrestle with concerns unique to your own unfolding family story.

Much of the book will talk specifically about same-sex sexuality, and yet our findings are also relevant in many ways to LGBTQ+ experiences more broadly—and we make specific applications to gender identity (transgender and other diverse gender experiences) in each chapter. The rationale for this is that there is more research available on the experiences of parents of gay children than there is of parents of transgender children, and the primary conversations in the Christian community have been around same-sex sexuality and behavior. However, we do see growing awareness of and interest in gender identity, and we include the gender conversation as appropriate.

In this chapter, we will share with you the experiences of Christian parents as they first became aware of their child's same-sex sexuality. We refer to this component of the parents' journey as *awareness*. Subsequent chapters will consider other components of the journey: what it means for parents to simultaneously seek help and maintain their relationship with their child, how this relationship changes over time, how parents' faith changed over time, and what it means for parents to come to terms with the reality of their child's same-sex sexuality. Since awareness chronologically precedes these other components of the journey, we will begin there.

Awareness can come through *disclosure*, as when a child like Lorelei shares the reality of her same-sex sexuality with her parents. Disclosure might take the form of a letter, a conversation, or an answer to a question that's been asked. Any context in which your child shares with you the reality of their sexuality is a form of disclosure. While some children may disclose their experience using only descriptive language—that is, by speaking of their attractions to the same sex—they will likely refer to themselves using a sexual identity label such as *gay, lesbian, bisexual, bi-curious, asexual,* or *queer*. A child might choose to disclose their sexuality to their parents after coming out to another individual who insists that the child tell their parents (or threatens to do so themselves). This circumstance is also a form of disclosure, but it differs from other forms of disclosure in that the timing of the disclosure might not be the child's preferred timing.

Awareness can also come through *discovery*, as when parents discover that their child is gay without the child intending for them to know. Parents might stumble across pictures on social media or be told by a friend or family member. One mother we saw in our clinic confessed to going through her daughter's bedroom when her daughter was at school and discovering her diary. The mother made the decision to read the diary, and that was how she learned about her daughter's sexual identity. We do not recommend this kind of action, as it jeopardizes the trust you want to have as a parent with your child. Regardless of how *discovery* occurs, it is a very different experience of awareness from *disclosure*.

From the child's perspective, disclosure is commonly referred to as "coming out," a shortening of the phrase "coming out of the closet." The image of the closet is an apt metaphor for many LGBTQ+ children, especially those in Christian settings. These children have often felt isolated from their parents, feeling the need to keep a part of their experience hidden away. Disclosure at the child's own pace, at a time that feels safe, is very different from being forced to disclose—as when a family member or friend threatens to tell a child's parents about the child's sexuality if the child does not do so. And both of these forms of disclosure are very different from the experience of discovery, particularly if this discovery entails a breach of trust and privacy.

The process of disclosure to others typically begins with an LGBTQ+ person's friends and peer group, often during adolescence. This is thought to be the safest group of people for most teens to disclose to. However, responses to coming out are quite variable, with racial and ethnic background sometimes playing a role. In a study by Aranda and colleagues, for instance, African American lesbians were less likely to disclose to a nonfamily member than were whites and Latinas in the study, suggesting that comfort levels among different groups may vary for reasons not yet fully understood.[1]

In the most typical coming-out progression, after telling one or two friends, an LGBTQ+ person discloses to more friends, and word spreads to the rest of their peer group. After friends and peers, the person they are most likely to come out to next is a sibling, then their mother, and finally their father.[2] We found this pattern to be true in a recent study of Christians who have come out to their parents.[3] Fathers need not feel offended if they are the last to know about their child being gay; it appears to be a common experience. Perhaps in some families there is something about being a father that represents a more daunting task. We don't know. There are exceptions to this pattern, of course, and it applies only to controlled disclosure of a person's same-sex sexuality, not to discovery of their sexuality by others. Christians who come out are also likely to disclose their sexuality to youth ministers, who in the typical coming-out chronology fall between friends and siblings. These youth ministers seem to provide another layer of anticipated safety for some teens along the journey of eventual disclosure to their family.

In our most recent study in which 125 Christian parents reflected on their experience of a child coming out to them, about half (49%) suspected their loved one was gay before their child came out to them, while 51% had no idea. One parent who had suspicions shared, "Over the years I had wondered if he might be gay because of some effeminate behaviors and his lack of interest in dating during his teens." Another parent shared, "He had dropped some hints, but I didn't respond to them, hoping I was misreading him."[4]

Among those who had no idea their child was gay, one mother shared, "There was absolutely no indication that either I or my husband ever noticed." Another parent shared, "I just never saw it. She was focused on college and really didn't have time to date. I felt she was just waiting for the right guy to come along."

Coming out occurs in the social and cultural context not only of family but also of race, ethnicity, kinship networks, and (for many) a religious faith community. Differences among these contexts can contribute to very different experiences when coming out. For example, in a study of gay youth, Black youth reported increased discomfort coming out compared to White youth, and Black and Latino youth disclosed to fewer people than did White youth.[5]

The coming-out literature is layered with complexity that we want to keep in mind as we think about how a Christian parent responds to their child's disclosure as gay.

Before we discuss reactions to coming out, we want to introduce a diagram that will help us locate various ministry considerations throughout the book (see fig. 1.1). What we illustrate here is that, after parents become aware of their child's same-sex sexuality, whether via disclosure or via discovery, two parallel journeys occur. One is the journey of the child who has come out or is navigating sexual identity questions; the other is the journey of the parents, who are now aware of their child's same-sex sexuality. We will look in subsequent chapters at how this relationship changes over time. These two journeys are not always best conceptualized as completely separate, but there are ways in which they each have their own terrain to navigate, as we shall see.

> *Two parallel journeys occur: the child's and the parents'.*

REACTIONS TO COMING OUT

Most parents are uncertain how to react when a child comes out to them. Parents report a wide variety of emotional responses, many of which can be quite negative, such as shock, grief or loss, guilt, shame, anger, emotional withdrawal, and even verbal and emotional abuse.[6] This means that just about anything can happen, and you can play a role in how your story turns out. Support and acceptance are also reported, but less frequently. As you will hear from parents who have gone through this before you, you have an opportunity to rise to the occasion.

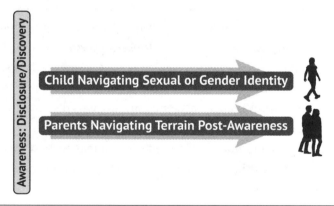

Figure 1.1. Two parallel journeys

These initial reactions by parents are frequently followed by a period of distress and finding ways to cope or adjust to the news they have just received.[7] We will return to parents' coping responses in chapter two. For now, we want to focus on parents' initial reactions, specifically the experiences of Christian parents.

While every parental response is complex and individual, it can be helpful to broadly classify parental reactions as either positive or negative. Psychologists tend to classify reactions this way—as positive or negative—to people you understand that their reactions matter. They can move toward something constructive (of emotional health and well-being), or they can move away from that toward something that can be destructive (of emotional health and well-being). Don't confuse "positive" and "negative" with "affirming" and "nonaffirming"; those are going to be different issues with some overlap, of course, but we are talking primarily about the impact on health and relationship. Some studies find that about half of parents respond positively to their child's coming out (by demonstrating support, for example), while the other half of parents respond negatively (through behaviors such as verbal harassment or worse).[8]

In one of our recent studies of Christian college students who came out to their parents, about 24% described coming out to parents in strongly positive terms, 28% in strongly negative terms, and 44% in a mixture of positive and negative terms.[9] One student who experienced a mixture of positive and negative responses when disclosing their sexuality to their mother wrote, "There were positives and negatives. . . . It was very much okay . . . but we're not going to deal with it. . . . She never brought it up again."[10]

What internal reactions do parents experience as they respond externally in positive or negative ways to their LGBTQ+ children? We found in one study of Christian parents that grief and shame were very common experiences.[11] Indeed, religious commitment and grief were highly correlated. Perhaps more encouraging is the research suggesting that many parents typically experience positive growth after the disclosure, and most parents grow more accepting of the circumstances their family faces and of their child over time.[12]

What contributes to some parents' reactions? Other research has focused on variables that commonly underlie parental reactions to their child's coming out. Family, religious, and cultural values are all associated with parental reactions.[13] What we found in one of our earliest studies of Christian parents was that their responses were related to their Christian worldview, a sense of ambiguous loss, emotional distress, and also unique situational stressors.[14] What do we mean by each of these terms?

Christian parents have much in common with nonreligious parents, but one thing that stands out in some studies is what we refer to as a "worldview" response. A worldview is the sum of assumptions a person holds about what is true, and a Christian often holds a distinct worldview that undergirds and organizes their beliefs, values, strivings, and other considerations. Beliefs about what is right and wrong, about morality and sexual behavior, about what God provision for a person, and other things like these would be a part of this response. Worldview can interact with and be expressed in relation to other aspects of parents, such as differing ethnic and racial backgrounds.[15]

Parents also reported ambiguous loss and emotional distress. Ambiguous loss is more of a free-floating sense of something not being the way a parent thought it would be. If you are a parent who feels a sense of loss but doesn't know quite where to pin that loss or where to locate that loss, that's what we are talking about here. It is a vague sense of loss that isn't so much directed at your child or at God or at anyone in particular, which can sometimes make it hard to name and hard to work through.

Emotional distress would be tied to largely negative emotions. These might include ambiguous loss but would also involve common feelings of confusion, anger, frustration, guilt, and so on. Situational stressors just refer to unique situations that will vary from parent to parent. One set of parents will learn that their child is gay, while another set of parents will learn that their child is gay and sexually active. Or one set of parents finds out their child identifies as transgender, while another set of parents find out their child is transgender and now insists on the use of cross-sex hormones. The situation is different and creates additional stress. These are what we refer to as situational stressors.

There are additional considerations discussed in the literature. Two variables that make parents more likely to respond positively to a child who comes out are (1) education about sexual identity and orientation, and (2) previous contact with sexual minorities or the LGBTQ+

community through extended family, friends, and coworkers. Conversely, parents are more likely to respond negatively if they have had little exposure to LGBTQ+ individuals and communities or if they have strongly ingrained stereotypes.[16] A practical implication of this is that it really is worth learning all you can about the issues—as you are doing in part by reading this book.

Other variables that influence parental response include the nature of the information shared by the child (for example, if they are in a relationship), the method through which parents become aware of the fact that their child is LGBTQ+ (that is, whether they learn through disclosure or discovery), and the sex of both parent and child.[17]

How thoughts are tied to feelings. Some research suggests that parents may have specific cognitions (or what you might think of as mental actions, thoughts) that affect their reactions.[18] These thoughts include concern for their child, whether their child is abnormal, whether their child will change, and what their child's future might look like. Parents may blame themselves, or they may have a sense of pride in who their child is.

Here are common thoughts held by parents at the time of disclosure:[19]

- concerns tied to safety, negative social attitudes, prejudice, and harassment

- concern for the future and worry that their child will have a harder life (being lonely or unhappy)

- concern that their child will not have children, meaning that the parent will not have grandchildren

- self-blame and belief that they have failed as parents

Other research, ours included, suggests at least two additional beliefs may be common among religious parents, making them especially important for this book:

- concern that their child will lose their religious faith

- conflict between the parents' love of their child and their religious beliefs and values

In our own analysis of data from more than two hundred Christian parents who had a child come out to them as gay, we noted several themes. Some of these themes are reflected in the broader literature about parents, while other themes seem to be more prominent among Christian parents or more closely tied to the Christian beliefs and values held by Christian parents.

JEAN COLES ON HER FIRST AWARENESS OF HER SON'S SAME-SEX SEXUALITY

Greg came out to us when he was twenty-five years old. I wasn't totally surprised. Occasionally throughout his life, I'd wondered if he might be gay. At the same time, I'd assumed that he was straight. And I'd prayed that being gay wouldn't be something he would have to deal with. It seemed to often be a life filled with angst, loneliness, and hardship, as well as ostracism and unfilled desire. And that's for those who choose not to act on their desires! I was sad to learn that this road was one he would have to walk, but confident that God was in this and would walk it with him.

When he told us, we were quick to listen and affirm our love for him. We also asked questions, seeking to understand his journey and help him feel loved and accepted. We let him know that he didn't need to answer our questions unless he wanted to (which he did). I told him that I would be praying three things for him: to always (1) have healthy belonging with godly intimacy, (2) use his gifts without hindrance, and (3) not experience unhealthy shame.

Additional Christian considerations. One of the most frequent (and perhaps most obvious) concerns Christian parents reported had to do with whether homosexuality is sinful. A second closely related concern was the question about what their child's homosexuality meant for the child's relationship with God. These questions are often multilayered, in large part because the term *homosexuality* can refer either to same-sex attractions or to same-sex sexual behavior. Some parents were concerned only with the sinfulness of same-sex sexual behavior. These parents might not have viewed same-sex attractions as "good," but they did not view such attractions as morally impermissible in the same way they viewed same-sex sexual behavior as sinful. They saw attractions distinct from behavior. For other parents, both attractions and behavior were considered sin. Still other parents did not view homosexual attractions or homosexual behavior as sin, or they were questioning those beliefs.

Among those parents who considered homosexual attraction or homosexual behavior sinful, some viewed that sin as no different from any other sin. Other parents viewed homosexuality as uniquely sinful, putting their child at spiritual risk in a way other sins might not do and threatening the child's salvation.

One Christian parent we interviewed shared the following response to her daughter's coming out. Her recollection captures both the love she expressed toward her daughter and her beliefs about what God thought: "Basically, I remember it was just like putting a knife through my heart. I remember crying a little bit. I told her that she was my daughter and that I would always love her, but I did not personally believe this was what God would want for her and I did not want this to come between us."[20] This kind of response may also confuse a parent's questions about what choices their child has made to be gay. We believe it is important for parents to give careful thought to what is volitional—that is, what their child has say over. In our experience, people do not choose to experience same-sex attractions. Rather, teens who may later identify as gay typically find themselves experiencing same-sex attractions when they go through puberty. When parents talk to their child about what God may want for the child, it is important not to frame this conversation in a way that suggests the child chose to experience their attractions. Parents sometimes respond to their child's coming out by expressing concern over a choice the child is making in contradiction to God's best for them. Such a response is often quickly rejected by the child—whose attractions usually developed unchosen during puberty—and will create a wider divide in any effort to convey respect for the child or to achieve mutual understanding.

The belief that homosexuality (whether simply same-sex sexual behavior or same-sex attraction as well) is a sin can also be related to beliefs about how best to respond to a child. A common theme among Christian parents is the belief that same-sex attraction can or should be changed. Some parents considered ministry or counseling efforts to facilitate change, while others spoke of their child's attractions as a possible phase that the child needed to grow out of or as some sort of confusion on the child's part. Regarding counseling efforts, one parent said it this way:

> I was really in denial for a long time. I said, "We have to get this thing fixed." I figured [our daughter's same-sex sexuality] had to be something psychological. We pushed [our daughter] to go into some Christian counseling with somebody that specialized with the SSA lifestyle but she was against that. She was already resigned to this was the way she is and how it is going to be. That made me even more angry.[21]

Parents' beliefs can fuel concrete steps that may backfire, as in this case where the parent tried to arrange therapy, which the child refused. Conflicts such as this can contribute to further anger on the part of the parent.

In our research, we heard less frequently from the subset of Christian parents who believed that neither same-sex attraction nor same-sex sexual behavior was sinful. For this group of parents, religious belief played a very different role in informing parents' reactions to their child coming out. Not every Christian parent will begin from the same ethical conclusions. Christian parents may reflect a range of beliefs and values about sexuality and sexual behavior.

WHEN A CHILD COMES OUT AS TRANSGENDER

Although most of our research is on Christian parents whose child came out as gay, we have always had a small percentage of Christian parents share their experience of a child coming out as transgender. What was their experience like?

One thing we found in our initial study of over two hundred Christian parents was that the parents who reported a transgender child were less likely to be surprised at the coming-out moment. Most of the study's cases of gender dysphoria were what we refer to as "early onset"; that is, the child expressed a different gender identity through sustained gender-atypical behavior, dress, and other preferences at a young age, prior to puberty. A child is typically aware that they are a boy or a girl between the ages of two and four, so early onset cases of gender dysphoria will often stand out to parents in important ways. In our research, these parents knew something was going on, even if they didn't know what it was at first. By the time their child grew up and came out to them as transgender, they were not as surprised as those Christian parents whose child came out as gay.

In our more recent research and consultations, however, we are seeing a dramatic increase in "late onset" cases of gender dysphoria— cases that begin after a child has gone through puberty. Many people who experience late onset gender dysphoria have little or no history of gender-atypical interests, behavior, or expression in childhood, so when they come out to a parent, the parent often reports feeling "blindsided." This feeling can lead to strong emotional responses: shock, confusion, concern, fear, and so on.

One of the more common responses by Christian parents when their child came out to them as transgender was an emotional response of grief or anticipated grief over the loss of their child as they knew them. One parent shared, "In the first couple of conversations we had, I did a lot of crying about feeling like I was losing my son. [My transgender daughter] kept saying, 'Mom, I'm the same person.'"[a]

Other Christian parents saw their child's transgender experience as a reflection of congruence. That is, these parents were aware their child was different, but they did not understand the nature of that difference until the child came out to them as transgender. For example, one mother of a biological male whose gender identity is female (a transgender daughter, as the mother would refer to her) shared,

> When she came out to us as trans, my first reaction was relief. I was like, "Oh, now everything makes complete sense." As I look back, I see, "Oh, there she is," whereas I wasn't sure before.... So she told us [she is transgender]. She asked if we were surprised and I said no. I said I was really glad for her. As she described it, it was a deeply spiritual experience for her. She felt like she heard God say, "My beloved daughter." It was

like a rebaptism, laying down the masculine and picking up the feminine, which was thrilling to hear.[b]

For some parents, their child's coming out with a different gender identity answered some of the questions the parent had already been asking.

EMOTIONAL RESPONSES/DISTRESS

Having looked at the initial thoughts of Christian parents, we want to discuss common emotional responses to a child's coming out, keeping in mind that thoughts and feelings are closely tied to one another. Generally speaking, we characterize the parents' emotional response as emotional distress, which we introduce previously. Emotional distress can be expressed as concern, fear, confusion, disbelief, anger, hurt, blame, or other emotions. Although we have also seen parents respond with positive emotions such as unconditional love, even these parents often experience additional feelings that, when taken together, reflect a degree of emotional distress.

Concern/fear. A common parental reaction to disclosure was to report concern for their child's future. Indeed, in our recent survey of Christian parents, concern was the most frequently cited emotional response, with 82% of the sample indicating this emotion.[22] This response is common for parents of all faith backgrounds, and it is equally shared by Christian parents. The parents we interviewed typically believed that their child's same-sex sexuality would have an impact on their child's life or the life of the entire family. One parent said this: "It was a sad moment. I remember my husband and I lying in bed worrying about what life was going to be like and how we were going to tell people. I never thought of the possibility of [same-sex] marriage. I never thought that there would be other Catholics with sons like this. I was very concerned. I worried about AIDS."[23] More specifically, some parents thought the disclosure would change the parent-child relationship. One parent recalled experiencing anticipatory grief for how their child's disclosure would change their relationship: "It was a time of grieving because I knew this was going to change our relationship with him forever. No matter which direction we went, this was going to change and affect our relationship with him."[24]

Another common theme had to do with worry for their loved one's future safety. One parent offered the following:

> I was afraid, as a mother, of violence that would come toward him and the depression that I saw in him because of it. I was fearful of what the outside world would do to [my son]. It brought it home as soon as he said, "Yes, I'm gay." I realized those problems were . . . things that I was going to be dealing with that I had pushed aside [in the past] and thought I didn't have to worry about. When I would hear it on the news, I would feel bad, but it was not a part of my life. That came right to forefront as soon as he said he was gay.[25]

Another parent said this: "From more of a civil approach, [I was] just concerned about, as an LGBT person, the discrimination he's going to face. Actually, the hatred he'll face."[26]

Concern and fear are some of the most common emotional responses to a child coming out. However, not all parental responses to coming out are negative.

Unconditional love. Another, and in some ways a uniquely Christian, response to disclosure is that of unconditional love. There are Christian

---

LYNN AND GREG McDONALD ON THE DISCOVERY THAT THEIR SON WAS GAY

Our suspicions were confirmed when Greg Jr. was seventeen years old. I (Greg) found gay pornography on his computer. After we confronted Greg Jr., he confirmed he was gay.

Instantly, I (Lynn) felt like someone punched me in the stomach. My fear and adrenaline were rising rapidly. I tried to keep together, but I just sobbed uncontrollably. I felt desperate and alone. Hope felt gone, but what I didn't realize was hope was walking with me every step of the way. At some point, it became clear that we did not have to have all the answers to our difficult questions to experience the comfort and hope in Jesus.

understandings of love, anchored in God's love for us in Christ, that can sometimes deepen the meaning and experience of love parents intend to live out with their child.

In our survey of 125 Christian parents, unconditional love was the emotional response with which parents identified second-most highly; 78% of parents indicated feeling unconditional love in response to their child coming out to them.[27]

When asked to explain what they meant by "unconditional love," some of these parents stressed God's unconditional love of their child, while other parents believed God called them as parents to love their child unconditionally. One parent put it this way: "We know that our role is not to judge our son but just to love him. It's not even our role necessarily to change him, but just to love on him in Christlike love and get our Christian friends to pray over him and let God lead in how he's going to deal in that relationship."[28]

Additionally, many parents stated that they needed to love their child unconditionally without any other specification:

> Your kid just took a huge big step. They said something giant to you, [so you should] understand that they're in a really fragile place. That's the moment to overdo it on the acceptance. You can be a jackass later. You can tighten up the reins later. You can go back on some of the super loving, acceptance stuff later. In that minute, that's what they need. They're terrified that this is about to be a nightmare, that they are about to fall off of a cliff. The most important thing right at that [coming-out] moment is taking care of [your child's] fears.[29]

For some Christian parents, their commitment to unconditional love even meant they were open to leaving their faith in order to love their child: "I remember distinctly thinking to myself that I would walk away from my faith if it meant I couldn't love my son. As much as my faith is a part of my life and who I am, I would have walked away from it in a heartbeat if it meant I couldn't love my son."[30]

We have seen that parents' emotional responses often include concern, fear, and love. We have also seen that the tension between these differing emotions can at times reflect a kind of heartbreak as well. The heart of many Christian parents is divided between love for their son or daughter and distress that may take the form of concern, fear, and other negative emotions. Another common emotion for parents is disbelief, reflecting their uncertainty about what is happening.

Uncertainty/disbelief. In the survey we conducted, just over half of our sample reported hoping that their child was confused or that it was a phase. Similarly, about 42% of parents reported feeling uncertain whether their child was confused, or whether it was a phase. For example, one parent said: "My reaction was pretty much disbelief. I was thinking and saying, 'You are only fifteen. You're not sure what you are yet. You are a confused teenager.'"[31]

Another parent said, "We were sort of thinking that maybe he was just curious. . . . I think we sort of assumed or hoped that he was just curious about his own puberty or his own body changes."[32]

It's important to recognize the significant role that uncertainty, disbelief, and wishful thinking often play for Christian parents whose child has just come out. Ultimately, parents will benefit from gradually coming to terms with the reality of their child's same-sex sexuality. That process may take days, weeks, months, or even years. It is a journey.

The next two common emotions parents experience both have to do with self-blame. The first is parents' self-blame for not knowing about their child's same-sex sexuality; the second is parents' self-blame for causing their child's same-sex sexuality.

Self-blame (for not knowing). In one study we found that Christian youth became aware of their same-sex sexuality at age thirteen on average; the average age at which they first disclosed that reality to another person was seventeen.[33] This means that, on average, a Christian young person will navigate questions around sexuality and same-sex attractions for four years on their own. When parents learn that their child has been navigating this terrain alone, they often blame themselves for not knowing about it:

> I cried. The hardest part for us was how hard it was for him to have held that in for so long when he knew we would be loving and accepting. I struggled a lot and still do with how much hurt he has

had to live with because he didn't feel he could tell us sooner. I wonder what it must be like to walk in his shoes for a day. Our whole family was always accepting. I was hurt for him.[34]

The sadness this parent describes is not uncommon. Another mother of a gay son shared a similar anguish: "I didn't take any responsibility for [our son] being gay—I know you don't make someone gay—but how did I miss it? I found myself second-guessing everything."[35]

One mother put it this way: "As a parent you think, 'This is negligence not to have known this.'"[36]

A mother of a gay daughter shared about her own experience of depression and feeling overwhelmed by not knowing: "I was very depressed that my daughter had gone through this by herself for seventeen years. It just crushed me that I didn't know and I couldn't help her. For seventeen years my daughter hid a part of who she was from me. I thought, 'Oh my goodness. I don't even know my own daughter.' It was just a very overwhelming moment."[37]

A father contrasted his not knowing to his wife's apparent insights into the possibility that their son might be gay: "If I had been as sensitive to see what [my wife] had seen, it wouldn't have been as much of a surprise to me. I guess it made me feel bad a little bit that I wasn't as close to [my son] as I perhaps should have been [to realize that he was gay]."[38]

Sometimes the blame parents feel has to do with a belief that they have lost the opportunity to prevent this outcome. One father, reflecting on his gay daughter, shared that he wished he had known sooner in order to intervene: "I thought, 'Why didn't I see this at an early age so I could have corrected it as a young child?' There might have been some things I could have done. I had no idea. I was asking, 'What in the world did I do wrong?'"[39]

As this father's final words demonstrate, the self-blame parents feel for not knowing about their child's same-sex sexuality can sometimes be paired with self-blame rooted in a belief that the parents themselves are the cause of their child's same-sex sexuality.

Self-blame (as cause). Parents who struggle with blaming themselves for their child's same-sex sexuality are often responding to a common theory of causation subscribed to by many conservative Christians. According to this theory, a child attracted to the same sex must have experienced a failure to identify with their same-gender parent, creating an emotional longing that later became sexualized. Although we do not subscribe to this theory, we see many Christian parents struggle with questions about whether they were present enough or invested enough in their child's life. They often wonder in particular whether the same-gender parent was close enough to their child to meet these emotional needs that, according to this theory, should have ensured heterosexuality if they had been met.

For example, a father shared, "The biggest concern for me was, 'Is it something I did as a parent that caused hurt inside of him that led him to have these feelings toward the same sex?'"[40]

Another parent said, "I needed to find a reason why [my son was gay], and obviously, I couldn't. When it came down to it, all I knew is that I loved him, and even though I didn't understand, I wanted to understand and I didn't want to lose my relationship with my son."[41]

Still other parents resorted to blaming someone or something for causing or influencing their child's same-sex attractions. Some blamed experiences of childhood sexual abuse. The majority of those issuing blame blamed themselves for either causing the same-sex sexuality or being negligent about it. One parent remembered:

> It was very painful. I was hurt tremendously. Everything that I had read blames the father [for their child being LGBT]. So, I was feeling an incredible amount of guilt, like a complete failure as a father. All those things were running through my mind. . . . I wanted to know if he was ever abused as kid or if I had caused this. Had I been neglectful of him or abusive to him in any way? I was really concerned as to what caused his homosexuality.[42]

Another parent had this to say: "I blamed myself. I thought I did something wrong that caused it. I thought I didn't love her enough or pay enough attention to her. I thought maybe something happened [to her]. I was worried about her future."[43]

Many sources can lead parents to accept blame for their child's sexuality. Some of those sources are held up in religious circles as authorities on sexuality and gender. Other sources come from within the parents themselves. The love parents have for their child can sometimes lead them to blame themselves for their child's sexuality or gender identity. Obtaining accurate information on the development of sexual orientation and gender identity is thus an important step for parents; we will return to this step in coming chapters.

Questioning God. As all of the parents we interviewed were Christians, finding spiritual meaning in their experience was very important to them. Different parents expressed this search for spiritual meaning in a wide variety of ways. Some felt that their child's relationship with God was more important than the child's sexual orientation and chose to focus on fostering that relationship. Others specifically stated that they were avoiding asking spiritual questions because they were afraid of what they might discover. Still others saw their child's coming out as an opportunity for spiritual growth or as a trial they had to overcome: "You depend on God so much in these times and you are digging deeper in your faith. You don't have it all figured out. You're trying to figure it out, but you're in this place of total dependency on Him to get you through. It takes a lot of prayer."[44]

Some parents stated that they were trusting God, either specifically (in the sense that they believed God had a purpose for their child and their child's sexuality) or more generally:

> [My faith has been] strong really. I guess because I'd gone through
> [this experience] with [my son]. I felt like the Lord was uplifting me.
> I still felt kind of in a hole, underneath a huge cloud. But it was like,
> "Okay. I know God is with me. He's still there with me. He's still
> in this hole with me. I know He's going to pull me out." [I felt]
> stronger in my faith, I would say.[45]

On the other hand, many parents struggled or questioned God: "It was a roller coaster. Some days I would feel at peace and trust that although I didn't know what God's plan was, I knew He had a plan and that we were a part of it. Some days I was just hanging on. There were times where I was in the pit of despair and wondering what the next day was going to look like. It was a tumultuous time."[46]

If you are similarly struggling, you are not alone. Many parents report questioning God, grappling with who he is and what he is doing. A mother of a gay son shared, "My three questions for God were, 'Why us? Why [my son]? Why now?' It was a period of very deep grief for me."[47] Similarly, a mother of a lesbian daughter shared, "I was wondering, 'Where does this lead me with my faith? Do I still believe what I do? Where is God in all this? What do I do?'"[48]

> *If you are similarly struggling, you are not alone.*

This struggle manifested in different ways. Some parents were angry at God for allowing their child's same-sex sexuality. Others wondered whether God could make someone this way or whether it was the child's choice, while still others questioned how God could allow this to happen:

- A father of a gay son: "We did everything we could as good Christian parents and then all of the sudden it was like, 'How could this be?' That was definitely a strong question at that point. Still is sometimes."[49]

- A father of a transgender daughter: "I thought, 'This can't be right. God makes us either boys or girls. There is no distinction or gray area in between.'"[50]

- A mother of a gay son: "I was trying to reconcile: If God doesn't make mistakes, and he made [my son] this way, then what is going on here? Could God have made a mistake? Does God design people to be bisexual or homosexual or heterosexual?"[51]

- A mother of two lesbian daughters: "For [my youngest daughter], it was a lot more difficult than it was with [my oldest daughter]. I didn't talk to her for three weeks. I went into a depression. I would come home from work and go into my room. I wasn't talking to anybody. I was more mad at God. I asked, 'Why are you giving me another gay child?'"[52]

We will return to the question of how Christian parents' faith changes over time in chapter five. For now it is important for parents to recognize that the search for meaning, and how God fits into this meaning, is a common response by Christian parents when a child first discloses their same-sex sexuality.

As we orient you to this journey throughout the book, we want to revisit the idea that there are two parallel journeys when a child comes out (see fig. 1.2). One journey is that of the child who has come out, as they navigate questions of sexual identity or gender identity. Ministry questions related to children who have come out are beyond the scope of the present volume; however, we believe that such a path should include space for that child to take their faith seriously, to take their sexuality or gender seriously, and to take the relationship between their sexuality or gender and religious faith seriously. The child's journey will be an attributional search for meaning, identity, and community.[53] They may benefit from time to examine what has been said about people like them—messages they have heard and internalized from their local faith community, as well as messages from the mainstream LGBTQ+ community, entertainment, and the media. They may also want to identify how these sometimes problematic messages could benefit from a thoughtful, prayerful, counternarrative reflecting their beliefs and values as they develop and live out a purposeful sense of identity. Again, we refer you to other resources for the care and ministry considerations that are part of that particular journey.[54]

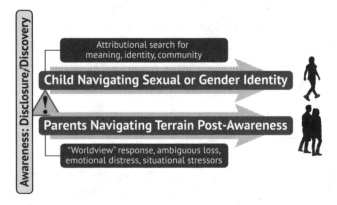

Figure 1.2. Two parallel journeys

DAVE COLES, ON HIS SON COMING OUT TO HIM

Our son, Greg, first told us of his orientation when he was twenty-five years old. At that time, we spent most of our time outside the United States. He did a great job of presenting us with the news, which I had not seen coming. He let us know in advance that he had a "serious" subject he wanted to discuss with us. We planned a phone call with plenty of time to talk and ask questions. We had a deep and satisfying conversation, with dozens of questions asked and answered. And we looked forward to face-to-face discussion a couple of months in the future.

As I remember it, two emotions dominated my heart—both in that conversation and in the months ahead. One was a sadness at the loss of a future I had envisioned for Greg. He had dated some wonderful young ladies, and I thought he would make a wonderful husband and father; I saw that dream of mine laid to rest. At the same time, though, I had a much stronger feeling of thankfulness and relief that he had grappled deeply with biblical teaching on the subject and landed on a position I could wholeheartedly affirm. Not only did his affection for Christ remain strong, but his handling of the relevant biblical texts reflected sound exegesis and submission to the teaching of God's word.

The second journey—the one that is the focus of this book—is the journey of Christian parents. In order to support parents along this journey, we believe it is necessary to understand their own emotional responses to their child. We have learned that many Christian parents have similar emotional responses and face similar questions as they navigate their faith commitments alongside concern and fear, love, uncertainty, disbelief, and self-blame.

WHAT ABOUT LGBTQ+ KIDS?

We have also studied the experiences of children who came out as same-sex attracted or LGBTQ+ to Christian parents. While these experiences are not the primary focus of this book, they can be instructive in understanding the journeys of parents. Participants in our most recent study of 229 LGBTQ+ persons recalled that, when they came out to their Christian parents, parents most often responded by expressing concern for their child's future; hoping that their child was going through a phase; expressing compassion, support, disappointment, and hurt; and blaming themselves.[55] This wide range of responses overlaps considerably with what Christian parents shared.

One participant shared how their parents were bewildered by their coming out: "They said they loved me, but they seemed confused; I knew it wasn't what they wanted. I felt I was letting them down."

Another person shared how his mother seemed fearful:

> The most obvious emotion my mom showed was fear. She also immediately tried to understand the causes of my attractions . . . she asked me about specific friends' influences on me. I don't know what my dad's response was, because I let my mom tell him when I was away at college because I was too scared of what his reaction would be. (I expected rage and punishment.)[56]

As this quote illustrates, parents themselves may not be on the same page as each other. This is crucial for both parents and those who support them to remember. Each parent may have their own emotional response and journey.

Some of our participants shared memories of how their coming-out experience led to shame and shaming. One person shared that their parents "asked me never to mention my homosexuality to anyone else." Another shared, "My father told my mother he wished I had just not told them." Similar, a participant remembers how, after she came out, her mother "angrily said she didn't want to know." Still other parents spoke of spiritual consequences; one participant remembers their parents telling them they were "going to hell and didn't really have a relationship with God."

About half (48%) of LGBTQ+ persons thought their parents already knew they were gay before they came out, while the other half (52%) did not think their parents knew. Interestingly, we saw a similar 50-50 split between parents who reported suspecting their child's sexuality and parents who had no idea. Some of our LGBTQ+ participants wrote:

They'd suspected for longer than I did, in retrospect.

They said that they suspected it when I was as young as twelve.

My mother already knew; my father didn't have a clue.

Mom said the possibility occurred to her, but she didn't know; Dad said nothing.

I had previously been caught on an LGBT discussion board online.

I broached the topic "What would you do if one of your kids was gay?" with my mother a few times before I came out. My father didn't truly suspect but was not surprised.[57]

ADVICE FROM CHRISTIAN PARENTS

As we bring this chapter to a close, we want to share three pieces of advice for Christian parents, offered by other Christian parents whose child has come out to them (and we will do this in every following chapter, too): *lead with love*, *accept your child and circumstances*, and *take care of yourself*.[58]

Lead with love. Most parents offered the advice that Christian parents should show unconditional love to their child who comes out to them. One parent put it like this: "Err on the side of love. That's what we're trying to do. If we look too accepting, it's because we're just trying to make sure that he always knows he is loved and supported."[59]

Another parent shared: "Know that [your] child's biggest fear is that you're going to reject them and not love them anymore—that just tears them up. If you can do nothing else, just love them through it even if you don't understand. Demonstrate that you're loving them, whether it's a hug, saying 'Let's go on a walk,' whatever. You have to demonstrate how much you love them."[60]

One way to lead with unconditional love is to reframe your child's coming out to you as an invitation to know them better. We often have parents say something like, "I don't know who our daughter is anymore. She came out last fall, and I don't even know her." When this happens, we often draw a line down the middle of a sheet of paper to create two columns. We ask the parents to describe their daughter to us, perhaps adding details we recall them sharing with us in previous meetings. We write down qualities such as "funny," "thoughtful," "loves Jesus," and "loyal to a fault." Then, on the other side of the line, we write "same-sex sexuality." We tell parents, "The fact that you now know this about your daughter doesn't mean these other qualities cease to be reflected in your daughter. In fact, you now have an opportunity to know your daughter better because she shared has something with you that you didn't know about previously."

This reframing can help parents focus on loving their child unconditionally. Children who come out to their parents want their parents to know them better, to understand more about them and about what they have been experiencing.

Accept your child and your circumstances. The second piece of advice offered by Christian parents was to accept your child and your circumstances.

The word *accept* can be difficult for some parents. *Accept* can carry with it connotations similar to the word *affirm*, which is often used in mainstream LGBTQ+ circles to reflect a celebration of all facets of same-sex sexuality, including affirming same-sex sexual behavior and marriage. We use *accept* more generally to mean "come to terms with the reality of what your child is sharing." It doesn't necessarily mean to "affirm" or "agree with." We will return to this concept in chapter six, as this shift from awareness to acceptance is a process and should not be overlooked.

Here is how one parent described the process of accepting their child's same-sex sexuality: "Remember that it's still your son or daughter. They are still the same person; you're just finding out something that you didn't know about them."[61]

Some parents offered practical advice for moving toward healthy acceptance while continuing to live out Christian beliefs, including particular actions to engage in or avoid. We will return to these recommendations in subsequent chapters.

For now, we want to share these words from a parent about the value of responding to a child's disclosure of same-sex sexuality by both extending and receiving grace:

I can sum it up in one world: grace. God gives us enormous amounts of grace every time we need it, and it's our responsibility to dispense that grace to those around us who have needs. Who has more needs than our own children? Dispense that grace to them in as many loving ways as you can. You'll be living out your faith if you do so. That is exactly what God wants us to do.[62]

If you are the parent of a child who has just come out to you, you will benefit from pacing yourself. Journeys take time. Emotional and spiritual journeys, in particular, take time. Work thought your own emotions and spiritual questions at an appropriate pace. Recognize that you may have a range of conflicting feelings that ebb and flow over time. You will benefit from pacing yourself. Journeys take time.

Take care of yourself. A final piece of advice to parents immediately after your child comes out is to make sure that you take care of yourself. When you are in crisis, pay attention to your basic physical needs. Make sure you are eating regularly. Make sure you are getting sufficient rest. Consider the benefits of exercise; even just walking on a regular basis can be helpful. Schedule breaks during your day. Identify a friend or two with whom you can talk and process your emotions.

Part of taking care of yourself is recognizing that the journey you and your child are on is indeed a journey. There is no quick fix, no three easy steps that can resolve all the challenges ahead. Each person's life is a story made up of many chapters; you have just learned important information about the chapter in which your child comes out. Many more chapters are still to come.

YOUR TURN: AWARENESS

Take some time at the end of this chapter to reflect on a few questions related to the coming-out experience as a Christian parent.

- How did you first become aware of your child's same-sex sexuality?

- How did the circumstances of your awareness (whether through disclosure or discovery) influence your response?

- What thoughts did you have at that time?

- What feelings did you have at that time?

- How were these thoughts and feelings connected for you?

- What were some spiritual questions you had, or questions you have today, that you are asking God to answer?

2

HOW PARENTS SEEK HELP

Ryan and Lauren, ages forty-eight and forty-six, came to counseling shortly after their daughter, Ashley, age twenty-two, had come out to them as lesbian. Ashley disclosed to her parents during her senior year at college, explaining that her roommate of two years was actually her girlfriend. Ryan and Lauren were upset; they felt deceived, having previously been told by Ashley that she and her girlfriend were "just roommates." Ryan and Lauren were disoriented, too, by some of their previously unspoken beliefs and assumptions about sexual orientation and attraction. They were disappointed that their daughter, who was "raised in the church" and "raised to fear and love God" would "do this" to them. When asked about their last contact with Ashley, Ryan and Lauren shared that it had been "a couple of weeks" since they spoke on the phone, and they weren't in a hurry to reconnect. They weren't sure how to respond and felt that their heads were spinning. They thought that seeking a counselor could be a good place to begin. Between the two of them, only Lauren had confided in a close friend. Neither felt comfortable telling anyone in their family or extended family; nor did they feel comfortable speaking with their pastor or associate pastor about it just yet. When asked about this, Ryan explained that he hadn't heard their pastor say much from the pulpit about gay people, but what he had heard made him wary of whether their pastor would know how to help them.

Although parents respond in many ways after becoming aware of a child's same-sex sexuality, we often see parents' actions directed toward two broad parental tasks post-disclosure: *seeking help* and *maintaining the relationship* (see fig. 2.1).[1]

AVOIDANCE VERSUS APPROACH

What does it mean to seek help? Alison Chrisler's model of parental reactions to coming out defines seeking help as one of four categories of parental coping strategies.[2] For Chrisler, coping strategies either move away from the reality of the disclosure (*avoidance*) or move toward the reality of disclosure (*approach*). These avoidance strategies and approach strategies can occur either in a parent's thoughts or in a parent's behaviors. Chrisler's four categories are cognitive avoidance (not thinking about it), behavioral avoidance (not talking about it or acting on it), cognitive approach (thinking about it), and behavioral approach (talking about it and acting on it). This final category, behavioral approach, is what Chrisler calls help-seeking. Help-seeking in this model is a coping response that *moves toward the reality of the disclosure*, and it encompasses *talking to others and collecting information* on parenting someone who identifies as gay.

> *Seeking help means different things to different Christian parents.*

Like Chrisler, we see help-seeking as an effort to engage the reality of the disclosure event, the new normal, an attempt to cope with greater knowledge, understanding, and meaning. In our view, seeking help means different things to different Christian parents. It often includes things such as obtaining social support, which invariably involves talking to others. But it also includes activities that both involve and exceed talking: identifying spiritual resources for support and guidance, for example, and going to counseling. Seeking help also often includes identifying helpful readings, podcasts, videos, documentaries, and other related resources. These resources might be specifically about parenting a child who identifies as gay, or they might discuss more generally the meaning of sexual orientation, theories of etiology, the likelihood of sexual fluidity or orientation change, how their religious faith views the topic, and much more.

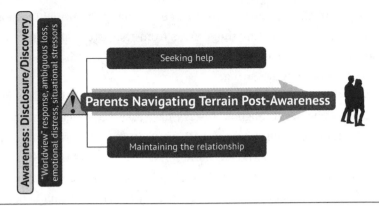

Figure 2.1. Two parental tasks post-disclosure

Seeking help includes identifying people whom parents can trust with their family's journey. In our research and clinical experience, it is difficult for Christian parents to find people in their faith community who can support them. Parents in evangelical Christian subculture whose child comes out as gay often seem to face a unique experience of shame. This shame can also be present to varying degrees in ethnic communities and cultural contexts that place less emphasis on the individual and more emphasis on families and communities. When a child comes out in any of these contexts, parents and families often face their own "coming out" experience.

Shame is an emotional response to the belief that (1) there is something fundamentally flawed in you (or someone close to you), (2) that you are in some way responsible for that flaw, and (3) that if others knew about that flaw, they would judge and/or reject you.[3] We often see conservative Christian families experience disproportionate amounts of shame when a child comes out. This shame appears to be implicitly or explicitly tied to the belief that parents do something (or fail to do something) that causes a child to be gay—a belief especially prevalent in evangelical Christian subculture.

Greg and Lynn McDonald, ministry leaders and authors of *Embracing the Journey*, have said that, in evangelical Christian circles, when a child comes out of the closet, the parents go into a closet. We have seen this dynamic at play in many Christian settings. It reflects the evangelical

Christian subcultural shame we noted above. Many parents will respond to this shame by isolating themselves from the potential support and resources that could otherwise help them manage the challenges, pain, and confusion they are facing.

Where does this shame come from? First of all, we need to remember that human beings throughout history have assigned religious blame for circumstances outside our control. We read in John 9 that Jesus' disciples asked him about a man who was born blind: "Rabbi, who sinned, this man or his parents, that he was born blind?" (John 9:2). It was common in that day to assume blindness was caused either by the sin of the blind person or by their parents' sin. Christians today are not far removed from similar assumptions. We often blame the person who is gay—as though they chose to experience same-sex attraction—or blame their parents for doing something or failing to do something that caused their child to be gay. Although no one knows for certain what causes sexual orientation, we suspect the Christian tendency to blame parents is an artifact of some early psychodynamic theories of causation suggesting that same-sex sexuality is the result of unmet emotional needs for a same-gender parent.[4] There is little research support for this dynamic as a cause of same-sex sexuality or a homosexual orientation. The theory still lingers in evangelical circles, however, often to the detriment of Christian parents who are desperate for help but feel constrained in sharing their needs with others.

Shame can also arise in relation to cultural factors that influence health and well-being. For example, some Asian American families—depending on factors such as age and acculturation—may emphasize the family unit over the individual, expecting that the needs of the family will be prioritized over the needs of any individual within that family.[5] There may be added barriers in these families to seeking out help, and families may deny concerns or remain silent about them unless they are directly asked. In addition to their potential challenges, however, cultural contexts such as these can also provide potential advantages such as traditional teachings, philosophy, anecdotes, and history.[6]

Let's return to the church, a potential resource to which parents are often reluctant to turn for help after a child comes out. Although these parents may very well stay in the church, they often feel shame and may elect not to share about their gay child for fear of what might be said about their child or about them as parents.

Yet Christian parents who have gone before you would tell you to find people you can confide in. Perhaps you will find only a handful of people who can truly listen to you, but these people will be an important lifeline for you to turn to for support.

A CAUTIONARY NOTE

Help-seeking should be done with discernment and prudence. Not everyone who seems like a potential help will actually become a source of support to you as a parent. Many people inside and outside the church, after listening to your story, might simply pass it along as gossip rather than offering real support. In Christian circles, this gossip can take the form of prayer requests or prayer chains—steps that may seem appropriate on the surface but are not actually supportive unless parents (and, even more significantly, the child) are given the option to approve these steps.

Indeed, given the risk of evangelical subcultural shame and the fear of becoming fodder for gossip, we strongly encourage parents to demonstrate prudence in whom they talk to about their child's sexuality. When determining whether a person is trustworthy, listen to how they talk about other people and their circumstances. Listen for whether they had permission to share something as a prayer request or to place a person or family in a prayer chain. Listen for empathy and compassion. If someone is surreptitiously talking to you about others, you can be pretty confident that they will likewise gossip about you with others.

We also generally operate on the principle that a person's story is their own to tell. What we mean by this is that, when a child comes out to a parent, that coming-out story is the child's story to share with others (or to keep private) at the child's own pace. It is often helpful for parents to discuss in advance with their child how this story will be disclosed. They may end up negotiating who will be told, whether parents or the child will share the information, and so on. Our experience has been that gay children are often supportive of their parents telling others about the child's sexuality, so that the parents can receive much-needed support. However, the gay child and their parents may need to have a few conversations about these dynamics in order to get on the same page.

> *A person's story is their own to tell.*

WHAT IF YOUR CHILD IS TRANSGENDER?

There are additional layers of complexity for those seeking help when a child comes out as transgender, and these layers require additional discernment. You may be working with a mental health provider who has little experience with people navigating gender identity questions. You may be weighing diagnostic considerations: Is the diagnosis of gender dysphoria warranted? Are there co-occurring concerns, such as depression or an anxiety disorder? The potential (but poorly understood) link between gender dysphoria and other conditions, such as autism spectrum disorder, can add an additional layer of complexity when considering the appropriate diagnoses and treatment plans.

One mother of a transgender daughter described her challenge coming to terms with this complexity: "The first few months I just wanted to understand more because I didn't understand transgender. I thought to myself, 'Maybe she is just gay.' I was trying to understand the difference between gays and transgender. Transgender is a whole different category. I didn't know much about that so me and the family had to learn."[a]

You may also face unique and time-sensitive decisions. For example, parents of older children may face the question of whether to use puberty blockers at the onset of puberty. The difficulty of this question might depend on the degree of discomfort a child is reporting. Parents of teenagers may be asked by their teen whether they can make a social or medical transition. Social transitions typically involve changes in clothing, hairstyle, and such. Some teens may also request use of a preferred name and pronouns. Medical transitions entail the use of hormone treatment. We frequently hear parents express concern that, when they meet with mental health and medical providers, few providers seem familiar with conventionally held religious beliefs and how those beliefs inform parents' approach to decision-making as their child navigates gender identity.

There are also fewer resources available to parents of transgender children. The books, podcasts, ministries, and other resources designed for parents of gay children significantly outnumber the resources addressing gender identity. This remains true despite remarkable increases in recent years of young people reporting diverse gender identities.

TURNING TOWARD GOD

Help-seeking for many Christian parents includes turning toward God as a source of support. Recognizing that the circumstances are out of their control, parents feel a need to seek out God, grow in their capacity to trust in God, and express their concerns and fears to God. Many Christian parents shared with us that they turned to prayer and to Scripture as sources of support during their child's coming-out process and afterward.

The positive benefits parents experienced when they turned to God and sought out faith-based resources included feeling closer to God, expanding their understanding of their child, reducing self-blame and fear, and increasing peace and hope.[7]

Prayer in particular can and should be tailored to the moments of greatest struggle. Praying before talking to your child may be helpful, especially if your conversations have become strained. You can pray to see your child as God does, to love your child the way God loves your child, and to experience peace and freedom from aspects of past conversations that have pushed your buttons and caused distress. You might also find it helpful to read Scripture passages slowly, inviting God to speak to you through the passages you are reading and journaling about what God is saying to you at this time.

One parent offered the following advice on prayer: "The biggest, biggest piece is look to God through prayer. People will tell you all sorts of things from both sides, but let God guide you. That's going to take a lot of laying down yourself to be able to listen. I'm still not completely there. Our life is day by day and it's not just [our son] it's everything that the world throws at us."[8]

Other parents shared similar advice about leaning on God and waiting patiently on God's will, plan, and timing. Parents also found that the powerlessness they felt when their child came out could convey important spiritual lessons to them. Because they were unable to fix the circumstances they faced, many parents were led to rely on God in a new or fresh way. One parent shared, "You are powerless unless you become like a child. I now understand that means that a child is completely dependent on its father. I did not grasp that before. I just thought it meant that you had to be innocent, but it means to completely turn over all of this to Him. Tell Him, 'I trust you with it, in your time, not mine.'"[9]

Similarly, a parent offered the following thoughts about trusting God's purpose in order to move forward in your family's journey: "God has a purpose for [your child] just as He does for heterosexuals. Find that peace and all-knowing God and trust His love for you and your child and move forward."[10]

Parents who turn toward God often also find it helpful to evaluate their beliefs about same-sex sexuality and behavior and revisit some of their prior assumptions. One parent encouraged parents to challenge their previously held beliefs about same-sex sexuality. Although few Christian parents substantially changed their views about sexual ethics, the process of reconsidering their assumptions often led to greater nuance and empathy:

> What [of your beliefs] is meant to be a way of dispensing with [a difficult question] so you don't have to deal with it and can put it in a nice package? Challenge your Biblical beliefs. Go back and look at Romans, where we see for us as fallen people that to somehow highlight that someone else is more fallen than you is completely unbiblical. Challenge the belief system.[11]

It is not uncommon for Christian parents to turn to God as they are looking for help and support. When parents feel out of control, they often turn to God as sovereign over their circumstances.

LYNN AND GREG McDONALD ON SEEKING HELP

Fortunately for us, we sought help from our local church. Our pastor was . . . a wonderful man ahead of his time on this topic of how to respond to the news of having an LGBTQ child. We made an appointment to see him. He immediately cleared his schedule to see us. He listened intently and shared tears and hugs with us. [He] wisely told us that God loves Greg Jr. and that we should continue to love our son deeply, and encouraged us to be sure to love Greg Jr.'s friends at the same time. We didn't know what that kind of love looked like at the time, but we continued to move forward, seeking to love.

We also reached out to some close Christian friends we respected and shared our news. They were very kind and sympathetic but not helpful. Not that they didn't want to be helpful; they just didn't know how to navigate having an LGBTQ child.

Our next step was to get educated on the subject. We went to our local Barnes and Noble, among other booksellers, seeking out anything that was LGBTQ related. There was not *one* book on Christian families having a gay child. The books we did find were polarizing. The secular books were about celebrating being gay. The Christian books were not personal stories but based on how wrong it was to be gay and [people needed to] repent. Both sides often seemed to be filled with hate, and we were not interested in that. We were unsuccessful in finding anything as to how to navigate these choppy and uncharted waters.

WHEN TO SEEK COUNSELING

When should you seek counseling? Some parents will benefit from meeting with a counselor by themselves. You may find that the coming-out experience has taken a toll on you. Maybe you are feeling worn down, overwhelmed, depressed, or especially anxious. Maybe how you are feeling is affecting you at work or in other areas of life that are important to you. You may benefit from someone listening to you and working through depression or anxiety. Other parents may want an emotionally safe place to share and process their fears and concerns so that those concerns don't come out "sideways" in an argument with their child or lead to a kind of fear-based approach to parenting that they later regret. Sometimes your fears for your child or for their future can come out in unexpected ways, such as being easily irritated or especially short with them or others you love, and it can be helpful to have a place to discuss and work through what you are feeling.

We also recommend counseling when you find that communication has broken down and you are unable to share and listen as you did before. Sometimes it helps to meet with someone who has no skin in the game. This is a third party who is there to listen to you or to your child or to both of you together. A good counselor can ask your child questions that allow you to listen to them in ways that have not been easy to do at home if there has been conflict. A good counselor can likewise ask questions of you that allow your child to hear your perspective better, perhaps for the first time in a long time.

You could also benefit from counseling as a couple if you find that you and your spouse are reacting differently to your child. It is easy to become polarized, which we will unpack more in chapter three. But essentially one parent can become a more extreme expression of one emotion, such as anger or confusion, while the other parent can become an extreme expression of another emotion, such as love or protection. This can lead to conflicts *between* the parents. A good counselor can see this dynamic in play and help you work through it.

Finally, if anyone in the home does not feel physically or emotionally safe because of what is being done or said, we recommend you seek counseling to help with safety concerns.

ADVICE FROM CHRISTIAN PARENTS

We have seen how Christians report looking for help in relationship with others and with God. We have also seen how knowing others who are or have been navigating sexual or gender identity or are otherwise a part of the broader LGBTQ+ community was helpful to many parents. We offer now advice from Christian parents about finding the right kind of support from others, as well as advice about the importance of identifying reliable and trustworthy resources.

Where two or three are gathered. You may not be able to find a church that is supportive across the board. You may not be able to be part of a small group or home group that shows you the kind of support you need. But we encourage you to identity a handful of people who can support you and journey with you through this season. One parent advises, "Find at least one or two people who will support you no matter what and listen to you. There's a lot you want to get out, talk about, and process, but not everybody is good for that. You don't want to talk to just anyone; you want someone who will listen, let you process, and not start judging the minute they disagree."[12]

Find reliable and trustworthy resources. For many parents, help seeking entails finding answers to their questions by identifying reliable and trustworthy resources they can read or watch to help them understand the experience of their child. Indeed, seeking out resources and learning all you can is one of the most common recommendations Christian parents of gay kids make to other parents:

> Try to get educated. Decide what's going to be most important to you, because that's what we all do. In other words, what things are you going to orient your decisions and your actions around? Is it going to be maintaining a relationship with your child? Is it going to be a commitment to scripture as you see it and everything else will revolve around what your understanding of scripture is— whether or not it clashes with reality?[13]

As the above quote illustrates, learning is not just about mastering a topic; it is also about orienting yourself to that topic, identifying what is most important, and discerning how your priorities will guide other decisions and behaviors in the coming weeks, months, and years. We will return to this broad perspective on learning, which we see as a valuable frame of reference.

Some parents of LGBTQ+ kids identified resources they found helpful or unhelpful as they adjusted to the reality of their child's same-sex sexuality.[14] The resources parents most often found unhelpful were those that emphasized an ex-gay approach to sexual orientation.[15] That is, these resources emphasized movement away from same-sex sexuality toward attraction to the opposite sex. Among Christians, this ex-gay shift is often associated with sanctification. Proponents of an ex-gay approach usually espouse theories of causation that implicate past trauma or a failure to identify with one's same-gender parent. These claims often propose a corresponding path to heterosexuality through resolving the negative emotional consequences of trauma or addressing unmet needs tied to a parent-child emotional deficit. Parents who found these resources unhelpful also felt that other parent-blaming approaches—as well as Christian radio to the extent that it reflected those approaches—were unhelpful.

> *"To read other people's stories and journeys, that gives hope."*

The resources parents most often named as helpful were resources informed by, respectful of, and compassionate toward the experiences of LGBTQ+ people and those navigating sexual or gender identity, as well as the experiences of parents whose child had come out to them. These resources did not blame the parent, nor did they blame the child. They were more nuanced and supportive, positioning parents to love their child in more helpful ways.

While parents did find some useful resources, they felt that more resources were needed, especially educational books providing multiple perspectives, guides to first steps for parents, web-based resources, and stories of people's personal experiences. One parent shared, "To read other people's stories and journeys, that gives hope. When you read about a family who walked through it and came out the other end."

YOUR TURN: SEEKING HELP

Take some time at the end of this chapter to reflect on a few questions related to the first parental task following disclosure: seeking help.

- What steps have you taken so far to seek help for yourself?

- What additional steps are you considering?

- How might seeking help fill a need in your life at present?

- How have you experienced God during this season? Is God a potential resource for you at this time? If so, share more about that. If not, what could help bridge that relationship?

3

HOW PARENTS MAINTAIN
THE RELATIONSHIP

Lincoln and Niamey contacted our clinic when they discovered that their daughter, Maya, age sixteen, was gay.[1] They had recently confronted Maya after seeing social media posts and pictures that gave them reason to think she was gay. At first Lincoln and Niamey wanted to drop Maya off for individual counseling, but we were able to encourage them to participate in some counseling, too, so that we could try to improve strained family relationships. Maya felt her parents were "overreacting" to her being gay and to the posts and pictures on social media, and she was especially upset that they had invaded her privacy by looking through her bedroom and reading her diary. Lincoln and Niamey were upset that Maya had not told them about her same-sex sexuality. They told Maya that her sexuality was a sin and that Maya needed to "make better choices."

In the last chapter, we noted two common parental tasks post-disclosure. One is to *seek help*, which we discussed in relation to establishing and expanding social support, identifying helpful resources, and turning to one's faith community and to God.[2] Seeking help can also include participating in faith-congruent parent support groups.

The other common parental task we have seen in our research is to find ways to *maintain the relationship* with the child who has disclosed their same-sex sexuality (see fig. 3.1).[3] This chapter considers the challenges Christian parents face in maintaining relationship with their child. These challenges may be related to worldview conflicts, advice parents receive from others, or particular factors of a child's experience, including their age, whether they have a partner, and whether they are sexually active. We discuss these and other complicating circumstances below.

As we see in the case of Lincoln and Niamey, seeking help and maintaining relationship are often intertwined. As Maya's parents sought help from us, they were implicitly asking for and expecting support to maintain their relationship with Maya. The task of maintaining relationship often involves challenge and discomfort; Lincoln, Niamey, and Maya were all challenged in our sessions to move toward a more honest and mutually respectful approach to each other.

This challenge took many forms. For example, we challenged the assumption held by Lincoln and Niamey that same-sex sexuality was the result of poor choices—a kind of willful disobedience on their daughter's part—and that better choices would make the same-sex sexuality go away. This belief reflected wishful thinking for Lincoln and Niamey, but it was not a realistic way to think about the etiology of sexual orientation, nor did it provide a way forward for Maya. (That is, Lincoln and Niamey had reached a point of diminishing returns in simply saying to their 16-year-old, "Make better choices.") We discussed in therapy what psychologists know (and do not know) about the causes of sexual orientation, the likelihood of orientation change, and the natural sexual fluidity that may be present in some people. We explained the therapy model we use, which does not attempt to change a person's sexual orientation, and our rationale for this approach. We also challenged Lincoln and Niamey to respect Maya's boundaries and her privacy. We encouraged them to come alongside Maya, to hear her perspective and experience, rather than allowing fear-based parenting to drive them into disputation and criticism.

Maya, too, was stretched in therapy. She was challenged to think through not only her own beliefs and values but also those of her parents. We encouraged her to begin thinking about how to take seriously her sexuality, her faith, and the relationship between her sexuality and her faith. She was only sixteen, so we knew that the journey she was on was a developmental one. Maya would face a number of decisions in the years to come, and the relationship with her parents was one of the best predictors of her well-being over time. We wanted to do all we could to help them maintain the relationship.

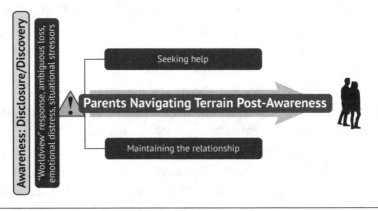

Figure 3.1. Two parental tasks post-disclosure

HOW DISCLOSURE RESPONSE LAYS FOUNDATION FOR ONGOING RELATIONSHIP

In our most recent line of research with Christian parents whose child came out to them as LGBTQ+, we focused on how the parent-child relationship changed over time. This question forms the focus of chapter four. In describing their relational evolution, however, many parents spoke about the importance of maintaining relationship with their child; these comments form the heart of this chapter.

A couple named Rossi and Deanna came in for a consultation about their daughter, age seventeen, who they suspected was gay. Their daughter hadn't come out to them, but she had previously responded to the topic in ways that made them wonder whether this was her experience. They were very anxious about the possibility that she might be gay, and they wanted to prepare themselves for what they believed was inevitable. They displayed a lot of what we might refer to as "anticipatory anxiety"; that is, they were anxious about the future, about things they anticipated would happen. To their credit, Rossi and Deanna wanted to get it right.

They wanted to be thoughtful and intentional about this moment. Rossi asked, "What should we say? How should we respond?"

As I thought about so many of the parents we have seen through the years and the data we have been analyzing from over two hundred Christian parents, there were number of things I wanted Rossi and Deanna to convey to their daughter if she did indeed come out to them. These are things I equally want other parents to understand as they interact with their own LGBTQ+ child. You see, how you respond as parents to your child's disclosure can put you in a better or worse position to maintain the relationship. Even if the moment of disclosure has already passed, understanding how your initial response has laid the stage for future relationship is an important part of discerning what next steps to take.

> *How you respond as parents to your child's disclosure can put you in a better or worse position to maintain the relationship.*

If you emphasize your love for your child as they are, reaffirming their dignity and worth in that moment, this will lay a better foundation for your relationship over time. If you thank them for sharing what they have been experiencing with you—even if they have not done so in the most helpful way this will lay a better foundation for your relationship over time. If you assure them that you will always love them and be in their corner, this will lay a better foundation for your relationship over time.

None of this requires that you agree with all of what your child has said to you. There are a number of potential complicating factors, as we will continue to explore. All we are saying at this point is that certain messages will lay a stronger foundation for your relationship to be maintained over time.

One parent shared the following about their child's coming out: "It was kind of a sacred moment, in a way. We all cried together. We just sat there and we told him we loved him. We said we would help in any way we could, thanked him for telling us, and heard what he had to say."[4]

Another parent shared, "I didn't know what to say. All I said was, 'I will try to understand,' and that my love for him would never stop. [I told him] that whether he was telling me that [he was gay] or not, I would always love him, regardless of what he was going through. I would be there to support him."[5]

Much of what parents shared with us offers valuable insight into maintaining a relationship. For example, one of the most helpful pieces of advice we can offer parents is to frame a child's disclosure as an invitation to know them better. Taking this hopeful view of disclosure may be counterintuitive. There may be various complicating circumstances that make it more difficult. The child might speak or act in ways that feel antagonistic to parents during the disclosure process. But one of the most helpful places you can begin is to commit yourself to seeing your child's disclosure as an invitation or opportunity to know them better than you did previously. Your child's disclosure represents a part of their experience you were unfamiliar with, an aspect of their experience that they felt needed to be kept hidden. Thanks to their disclosure, you now have an opportunity to support your child in this experience. As one parent shared with us, "The person you love is still there, and you need to support them just as you would anybody that you love."[6]

Getting to know your child better involves careful listening. Disclosure provides an initial opportunity for listening, and listening should continue over the next several weeks and months as you come to a better understanding of your child.

One parent explains how they sought to strengthen their relationship with their son after his disclosure:

A couple of days after [he came out] we went to be with him, because I didn't want there to be a feeling of distance because of this. The general feeling was tenderness towards him; there was no severing of our relationship whatsoever. If anything, I think I felt more of a need to be with him to try to understand it. I didn't want to be locked out of his world. I didn't want it to separate us from him at all.[7]

For some parents, their initial motivation to strengthen their relationship with their child results in a period of increased closeness that they compare to a honeymoon period:

> At first [my daughter] was incredibly lovey-dovey and clingy about it because it was okay [with me] and I think she was scared that it wouldn't be okay. My lesbian friend is one of the first people that I talked to. I told her, "[My daughter] just told me she's bi[sexual]." In talking to my lesbian friend about how I responded, [I realized] I probably need to dial it back and just let it be a nonissue. I'd gone a little overboard trying to let it be okay. At first [my daughter] really appreciated that I was trying to make sure it was all okay. There was actually a kind of honeymoon period there. [My daughter] was so relieved it wasn't an issue that it was kind of sweet.[8]

As this parent observed, a parent-child relationship after disclosure may be really good initially, reflecting everyone's efforts to go the extra mile with one another. The presence of an initial honeymoon period, however, doesn't mean that conflict will never arise later on. A child's coming out, or their ongoing experience of being out, may bring up other issues that generate conflicts. Disagreements are inevitable for any parent-child relationship. Regardless of whether there is a conflict at the point of disclosure, there may or may not be conflicts down the road tied to a child's same-sex sexuality or behavior.

One parent explained their conviction that responding well to their child's disclosure, and continuing to foster a strong relationship with their child, would be a form of Christian witness to others in their child's life, including friends from the LGBTQ+ community:

> The overriding priority was to communicate to [our son] and make sure he was aware that we still loved him. We did not want to do anything to sever our relationship with [him]. The primary importance was that nothing would come between us. We knew that a lot of [our son's] friends were watching us and they knew we were Christians. [Our son] told us later—when it all came out and we

were talking about it—horror stories of friends of his whose Christian parents disowned them. We were very determined not to let that happen. We thought, "We can work through this. No matter what, we need to love him, care for him, and be involved in his life."[9]

As we have seen, families have a lot to navigate in the moments during and following a child's coming out. For that reason, we want to home in on some of the common complicating circumstances we have seen that may make the coming-out experience and the task of maintaining the relationship a little more challenging.

BARCLAY JONES, ON MAINTAINING RELATIONSHIP WITH HIS DAUGHTER

I've always loved my daughter dearly, and nothing would keep me from wanting to maintain my relationship with her. God created her for his purpose and pleasure, not mine. She is a committed Christian, and to my knowledge she has not had an affair with another woman, so I haven't crossed a bridge many others have had to deal with. It is not a sin to encounter a sexual desire for other people—the sin is acting on that desire, whether straight or gay. Regardless, none of us are immune from sin. If she chose to enter a relationship with another woman, I wouldn't distance myself from her. How many people would disown a child who had a heterosexual relationship outside marriage? It's the same to me, and I am not called to sit in judgment.

COMPLICATING CIRCUMSTANCES

We want to acknowledge that every disclosure and subsequent effort to maintain relationship is unique. There may be complicating circumstances that place additional strains on the relationship. In this section, we will discuss how circumstances related to physical safety, dating and/ or sexual activity, unique aspects of your local community, and potential parent conflict can add complexity to relationship maintenance. Although this is not an exhaustive list, we have seen these themes come up repeatedly in our work with parents.

Physical safety.

When her sixteen-year-old son came out to her, Maria was confused and distraught. She had no idea that Hector was gay. A pastor at her church recommended a national ministry; she contacted them and shared over the phone some of what happened. They advised her to cut Hector off from any friend who was either also gay or in any way "supported his gay identity." She followed this advice. Hector became distraught and suicidal, and he eventually ran away from home. Maria called us to set up a counseling session in which she and Hector could meet to try to work on their relationship. In our first meeting together, Maria shared that she turned immediately to God in prayer after Hector came out: "No, no, no, God, please, help this not be so. Help Hector to turn to you, to turn back to you, and to follow your ways." She admitted later that she viewed Hector's same-sex sexuality as a kind of "willful disobedience" to God, which is why she prayed in that way. She also admitted that her prayer was offered up from a place of denial, wanting to believe that what Hector had shared with her was not true. Once Hector left home to live with a friend's family and Maria learned he was depressed and suicidal, her prayers shifted—she now pleaded with God to keep Hector alive.

The story of Maria and her son, Hector, involves a number of complicating circumstances that add layers of complexity to the coming-out experience. What was most challenging, of course, was the matter of physical safety for a son who was now depressed and suicidal, as well as old enough and impulsive enough to act on such thoughts. The advice of the parachurch ministry was unhelpful and in this case dangerous. Most mental health professionals do not recommend that people cut ties to social support without much more serious consideration, and never without adequate alternative support systems in place.

In this case, after meeting with us, Maria allowed Hector to reconnect with his friends, gay and straight alike, who supported him in his gay identity (a category that included nearly all of his peers). His depression lifted over the next couple of weeks, and he was no longer battling thoughts and impulses to hurt himself. Now we could work on the parent-child relationship; we could help Maria and Hector communicate with each other and consider what their relationship would look like now that Maria had this new information about Hector's experience of same-sex attraction. Physical safety is a prerequisite to work on relationship.

Some parents do not face concerns for their child's immediate safety, as Maria did for Hector, but they may still be concerned for the child's future well-being. These parents' protective instincts were sometimes activated by their child coming out to them. One parent shared, "I felt very happy that she could tell us and then very sad that she was going to have to deal with the world. It's hard enough to be straight in a straight world; it's really hard to be gay in straight world."[10]

Another parent offered a similar reaction rooted in her fear for her son's future: "I had a lot of fear for the future. What would it hold? Would he face discrimination? Would he potentially face physical issues as result? I felt fear for his safety, well-being, and emotional state."[11]

Dating relationships/sexual activity. Dating relationships and, in particular, sexual activity are the most common complicating circumstances we see that strain the efforts of both parents and their child to stay in relationship with one another. Such behavior highlights the moral objections parents may have about same-sex sexuality. Christian parents often have rules and expectations for all their children regarding waiting until a certain age to begin dating and waiting until marriage to have sex. But since parents who allow and encourage their straight children to date may be reluctant to do the same for a gay child, this raises questions about consistency and fairness. How can parents navigate with their gay child the expectation that children refrain from sex outside the covenant of marriage, if they do not believe same-sex marriage fits within a Christian framework of sexual ethics? And if parents typically allow their children to date after a certain age, what does this mean after a child has come out to them as gay?

One parent wrote to her daughter and tried to lay down some parameters for her daughter and her daughter's girlfriend in advance of an upcoming visit: "You know what we have done in the past when family or friends have stayed overnight and aren't married. We ask that you and [your girlfriend] would sleep in separate rooms. I know it probably seems silly, but we appreciate you going along with that."[12]

This kind of request could be met with mutual respect; the daughter might choose to honor her parents' values and not push back on this request, especially if she knows her parents would have made a similar request about sleeping in separate rooms had she been visiting with a boyfriend instead of a girlfriend. Since the mother has framed the issue in terms of the daughter and her girlfriend being unmarried, the daughter might wonder whether she would be allowed to sleep together with her partner in her parents' home if she and another woman were legally married. We have seen different parents respond differently to this question. We encourage parents not to commit too much to hypothetical future situations, as it is difficult to predict now how parents may feel about such a request in the years to come.

Your local community. Every family is located in a specific social and geographical setting. We have worked with families from the West Coast, the Pacific Northwest, the Midwest, the Northeast, the South, the Mid-Atlantic states, and so on. We have met with families from urban, rural, and suburban settings tied to each of these regions. Some of these communities are liberal or progressive; others are conservative or fundamentalist. Where you live will influence your relationship with your LGBTQ+ child.

Some parents, for instance, report being part of a small community in which derogatory comments were often made toward LGBTQ+ people. The hostility within these communities adds an additional layer of tension to parents' relationship with their child and the family's relationship to the community, especially once the child's sexuality becomes known by others in the community. These challenges can be exacerbated when family has a more public standing in the community, too. One parent remembered,

> In the initial months [after my daughter's coming out] I would have moments of weepiness and concern for her. Largely life didn't change. My beliefs didn't change. My understanding of my daughter didn't change. I wasn't shocked or trying to make her be something

she wasn't. I wasn't trying to talk her out of it. I realized what I would be up against. We live in a small community. My husband is an elected official. I have coworkers who speak in derogatory terms and bring up the gay issue regularly. I realized what I would have to deal with and how much rejection and what would happen. I wondered, "How out are we going to be as parents? Will we risk our careers? How far would it go?"[13]

Parent conflict and polarization. Another complicating circumstance occurs when parents are not on the same page about how to respond to their child. Parent conflict can range from simple differences in temperament (as when one parent is weepy and sad while the other parent is quiet and irritated) to major issues of emotional or physical safety. One parent shared,

I was terrified and embarrassed. I felt like it was my fault. . . . I was afraid of what her father would do and how he would react to her. Two days later, I had to step up in between them and tell him to leave the house because it got so ugly verbally. I stood up to him— which I had never done before—and protected her, even before I was okay with what she was telling me. I guess the mother in me came up and said, "You have to love and protect her. She's still a child and she's very, very fragile right now." I managed to make some good decisions even without all of the information and education that I have now. I do think that was a God thing. I was trying to do right thing, but I just didn't know what it was.[14]

It is imperative that parents protect their children.[15] Children need to be physically safe. The parent we interviewed above was right in observing that her daughter was "very fragile" and needed to be protected physically and emotionally as well as spiritually.

> *It is imperative that parents protect their children.*

In our experience, most parental conflict is the result of disagreements less extreme than this example. Parents often feel many conflicting emotions all at once. This mixture of emotions is called ambivalence. Ambivalent parents feel love for their child and also feel concern. They are protective and so, perhaps, fearful, but they are also confused. This ambivalence—these conflicting emotions—can lead to what we call *polarization*.

When parents are ambivalent, it is not uncommon for them to become almost caricatures of one of their emotional states. One parent might become exclusively focused on a positive emotion such as love, expressing this emotion by seeking to protect their child. The other parent may become polarized from their spouse by adopting a caricature of a negative emotional state such as confusion or anger. These emotions become more polarized as they interact with each other: The parent who expresses positive emotions such as love and protection is likely to express these emotions even more strongly as they see their spouse expressing concern or anger. Likewise, the parent who expresses concern will likely become even more concerned in interactions with the spouse who is focused primarily on love and support.

It is important for both spouses to understand when this dynamic is in play, so that they can resist the impulse to become polarized and express a caricature of their position. When we work with parents, we trust that both parents have both positive and negative emotions related to the coming-out experience, and we invite them to express and process the whole range of their feelings. Identifying, sharing, and processing their various positive and negative emotions can help spouses increase communication with one another, as well as facilitating their sense of cohesion and mutual understanding.

If you are a single parent, you may face additional challenges. Whether you are widowed, you have never been married, or you have been through a divorce, raising a child by yourself will present challenges. If you have been through a divorce, for instance, challenges may depend on the quality of your relationship with your former spouse. Perhaps the most challenging scenario arises when unresolved conflicts related to the reason for your divorce play into parents' response to a child who has come out. Arguments between spouses (or ex-spouses) may now center on how each of you is responding to your child—the child's coming out can become the stage on which current or former marital conflict is played out. It is important for parents to be aware of this possible dynamic. You will want to take a step back and work on communication and problem-solving skills that can be applied to a range of possible conflicts; these skills can then be applied to coparenting your child who has come out as gay.

LYNN AND GREG McDONALD ON MAINTAINING THEIR RELATIONSHIP WITH THEIR SON

Maintaining our relationship with our son was difficult for a couple of years. Both of us desired to stay connected, but our relationship had changed. We had made it clear that we believed it was wrong for him to have sex with another man, and we did not have to remind him of that, but we did.

I (Lynn) learned to weaponize the Bible and debated it with him at every opportunity. Those conversations strained our relationship even more. Our relationship felt like pushing together two magnets with the same poles. As hard as you try to put them together, they just won't. The more we talked, the further away I felt from him. It was a very sad time in my life.

After a while, our conversations were relegated to news, sports, fashion, and weather. We agreed to disagree on the subject of homosexuality. As you might imagine, our relationship felt empty, strained, and pitiful, but we wanted Greg Jr. to be in our life so bad. We held on to two absolutes. We were going to love God and love our son. We just had to figure out God's way of doing that.

WHAT IF YOUR CHILD IS TRANSGENDER?

Complicating circumstances when a child comes out as transgender tend to be related to the child's expressed desire to transition. The transition the child desires may include a different name, new pronouns, a complete social transition, the beginning of hormone treatment, or other considerations. Each of these changes can add great complexity to the steps you are taking to maintain relationship with your child. Yet the relationship you maintain is the best predictor of your child's well-being over time. This does not mean parents must say yes to every request, but we do strongly encourage you to walk with your child on the journey of figuring out their gender identity and expression and how that fits with your own faith.

One mother of a transgender son cited how her beliefs about the etiology of gender identity shaped her response to her son: "This is the way your child was born. Something in their life didn't cause them to be this way. It's biological and it's just the way it is. Hopefully no more kids have to suffer. Kids shouldn't have to suffer or lose their families or even feel like they've lost their family's support and love."[c]

For this mother, maintaining the relationship was anchored in her way of understanding her son's transgender experience (as rooted in biology), which fueled her compassion, love, and empathy.

Another parent had a similar response:

> I know one hundred percent that this is a medical condition. [My transgender son] was born this way. This is not a choice. When he first transitioned, I was still freaking out and wondering if this was a mental condition or a medical condition. Now my thoughts and feelings are one hundred percent supportive and I have a tremendous amount of love for transgender people of all ages.[d]

There is no single story here—no one outcome for families navigating gender identity and faith. Nor is there one answer to the many different circumstances parents are likely to face. For some parents, their ability to maintain relationship with their child has been closely related to their beliefs about what gender identity is and how it originated in their child, questions that are extraordinarily complicated. Because we do not know how diverse gender identities come about, answers to these and other questions will vary. Parents must grapple with how to respond to their child's gender experience, and their response may differ according to whether a diagnosis of gender dysphoria is warranted in their child's case, the severity of the dysphoria, the child's capacity to cope with the dysphoria, and many other considerations.

RELIGIOUS FAITH CONSIDERATIONS

Another challenging aspect of maintaining relationship for Christian parents whose child comes out to them has to do with how parents process their religious beliefs and values about same-sex sexuality and behavior. Many of the parents we interviewed expressed a strong love for their child, but they simultaneously held the view that homosexuality (whether same-sex sexual behavior or mere same-sex orientation) was a sin.

The fear about sin for many parents is a fear about potential eternal consequences. As one parent who had two lesbian daughters put it, "One of my first reactions was a fear of [my children] going to hell. That was my most terrifying thought at the time."[16]

Another parent offered,

I didn't know how to be a Christian mom of a Christian gay child. Everyone was telling me, "She can't be a Christian and be gay." I was thinking, "I'm a Christian, but I don't even know if I am acting like one. Maybe I don't know God's grace." It was a huge challenge for me. It was very confusing because I was confronted with my own prejudice and resistance towards her. I became this theological defender of the truth, which is something I don't like in other people. I'm not fond of people who think they are big defenders of the truth, yet I was becoming one of them. I was really discouraged about my own faith at that point.[17]

Although a number of parents shared the challenges associated with their religious beliefs, many parents also shared how maintaining a relationship with their child was a priority precisely because of their faith. In other words, many parents saw their relationship with their child as having a religious faith component to it. One parent shared how God spoke to her about what she should do in response to her son's coming out: "I said [to God], 'Help! We've tried on our own and it's not working and we need you.' God said very clearly to me, 'Just love [your son] and trust me.' So, I started actually trying to do that, because it was the only thing I had to hang onto—a lifeline."[18]

The commitment to maintain relationship is often complicated, especially as parents navigate conventionally religious beliefs and values.

One mother reflected on how this complexity played out in her own process with her son, who had come out as gay:

> He felt that I was hardened by [my Christian faith] and wouldn't be open to him being gay. I told him, "No, that's not the case. My gut feeling is telling me you can love God and be gay and that's okay." We both cried. He asked me, "What if I date a guy, can I bring him in front of my brothers?" I said, "Yeah, it's going to have to be, because I'm not going to lose a son over this."[19]

While questions about faith and sexual or gender identity can pose a tremendous challenge to parents, especially when they remain unanswered, this does not mean that faith is necessarily an impediment to parenting. Many parents cited their Christian faith as providing them the strength and motivation to maintain their relationship as a reflection of the love they had for their child, a love strengthened in many ways by the love they had experienced in their relationship with God.

> *Many parents cited their Christian faith as providing them strength and motivation.*

Just as parents must wrestle with the intersection of their faith and their child's sexual or gender identity, many LGBTQ+ children also wrestle with their own faith questions. This wrestling can also inform their parents' wrestling in turn.

Some kids will have wrestled with their faith and sexuality for some time before their parents even know about the struggle. As parents deal with their own religious journey, then, they may also be dealing with reactions from others in their faith community, as well as with the reactions of their child toward God. All these factors add layers of complexity to parents' journey with their child.

WHAT IF YOU GOT OFF ON THE WRONG FOOT?

All parents will make mistakes in their relationship with their child. The fact that we are discussing one of the most challenging topics families navigate only heightens the sense of regret parents may

feel for mistakes they made early on following their child's disclosure. Some parents have shared with us about their regrets and want
to offer their experiences as an important lesson for other parents.

Here is a mother reflecting on the ways she wishes she responded
when her son came out to her as gay:

> In those first few months I said a lot of things I regret. I never
> said, "You're going to hell," or "God doesn't love you," but I
> emphasized that it was wrong and that the only way to have
> a happy life was to either change or live a life of celibacy.
> One of my biggest regrets in life is my initial reaction in those
> first few months. I wish I had said, "No matter what I believe
> or you believe about this, I want you to know I love you. We
> are going to always have a good relationship. We are going to
> get through this. I know who you are. I know you are a good
> person. I know you are worthy of love and acceptance. I am
> always going to love and accept you." I wish I would have
> sent a loving, affirming message right then. Even though I
> believed same-sex relationships were wrong, there was a
> better way for me. What I think drove me was that the mes-
> sage from the church had made it seem like [homosexuality]
> was the worst thing in the world. My response was so fear-
> driven. It was not based on love. I wish it would have been
> different. Thank God that we've had the opportunity to move
> past that. [My son] has completely forgiven me. and we have
> a good relationship now.[a]

Another parent offered this advice: "Listen and love them and do
not be judgmental. I wish we would have said less about his lifestyle and more about how much we loved him and how proud we
are of him in general and not made him feel like we were ashamed
of him. I think judgment is the most painful thing. These kids are
enough in torment without us adding to their torment."[b]

You can see in both of these parents a wish that they could go
back and say less about certain fears or hesitations with their child's
"lifestyle," emphasizing instead their love for and pride in their child
and their commitment to the relationship.

If you've gotten off on the wrong foot with your child—if you said or did something at the moment of disclosure that you regret—spend some time thinking and praying about whether you could sit down with your child and express sincere remorse and ask for forgiveness. Don't try to justify your words or actions. If you regret them, apologize. Then say the words you wish you had said at the moment of disclosure.

ADVICE FROM CHRISTIAN PARENTS

What advice have Christian parents of an LGBTQ+ child given for maintaining the relationship with their child? In our previous work with parents, we've found two common pieces of advice that may be helpful for parents newly navigating this terrain: suspending judgment and having productive communication.[20] Let's discuss both of these pieces of advice.

Suspend judgment. The Christian parents we've worked with have told us that there are many things about their child's same-sex sexuality they did not understand. They faced many concerns and fears—including concerns and fears rooted in their religious beliefs and values—that were all rolled up in their reaction to their child's coming out. Working through these tensions often took a great deal of time. In order to maintain their relationship with their child in the meantime, parents found it helpful to suspend judgment and focus on the here-and-now relationship with their child.

One parent offered this advice to parents with ongoing theological questions and concerns who wanted to maintain their relationship with their child: "Suspending judgment [is crucial], even if it absolutely conflict[s] with your theological framework around the issue. It's way more important to suspend that judgment and love them and journey with them and keep a relational tie to them, than it is to have to be right about your convictions."[21]

As this parent's advice suggests, it can be helpful to conceptualize your child as embarking on an ongoing journey, which you as parents have an opportunity to join them on. The ongoing nature of the journey means that not every point of tension or conflict you feel needs to be immediately resolved. Joining your child on their journey and continuing to be a resource to them will require maintaining relational ties to them, which can be aided by setting aside judgment.

Another parent discussed her struggle with a well-worn evangelical phrase that she felt placed her in a bind: "My biggest struggle for the first couple of months with [my son] was, 'How do I love the sinner and not the sin?'"[22] The advice she gave to others wrestling with this same question—advice she ultimately applied to her own relationship with her son—was, "Take the focus off this issue and really love your child."[23]

BARCLAY JONES, REFLECTING ON HIS RELATIONSHIP WITH HIS DAUGHTER

Regardless of our desires for our children's lives, we only have a short time to love them and guide them. That is our role. Nowhere does the Bible list hatred or abandonment among the list of attributes God seeks in a parent to raise one of his uniquely created children. We need to know that God entrusts a child to our care for his reasons and that we may not understand those reasons in this lifetime any more than we understand his reasons for permitting suffering. My experience has been that my children have taught me that I don't have the answers and shouldn't presume that I do.

> "My children have taught me that I don't have the answers and shouldn't presume that I do."

Productive communication. The second piece of advice from parents that we see as directly tied to the task of maintaining relationship has to do with engaging in productive communication. Productive communication includes "listening to the child, engaging in conversations, asking questions about the child's experience, and keeping lines of communication open."[24] One parent shared her thoughts on what this process could entail:

Our [LGBT] children are overly sensitive to our responses and how we think about it, so I would encourage parents to emphasize your common ground, not the differences you have in your sexuality. Focus on the good things that they do and can do. Let go of trying to change your child. Show love and compassion. I don't think parents should change their viewpoints just because their child is that way. They should stand firm in their beliefs. Some parents might think, "If I change my beliefs, that would be better," but I think in reality [your LGBT child] would respect you less, in my opinion. Find common ground and show love and compassion. Stay away from divisive conversations about it, because I don't think it helps.[25]

This advice includes several layers. In this parent's experience, productive conversations involve finding common ground, placing emphasis on things the child does that parents can genuinely be excited about, and making the decision to not jump into conversations that you know will be divisive.

Other parents framed productive communication differently. For example, one mother underscored the importance of keeping lines of communication open. She felt that doing so helped her provide love and support, as well as reducing risk to her son:

We've tried very hard from day one to give love and support to [our son]. All those fears I mentioned at the beginning, I felt like our job now as his parents is to help keep him as safe as possible and to help him have less risk. To do that, we needed to keep the communication lines open. We needed to understand things better, which is why we were trying to educate ourselves as much as we could. We needed to have conversations with him about his story and things that he was encountering. There were many tearful phone calls that he'd make about some friend saying something unkind to him. We'd have to pick up the pieces. I just went into protection mode. I just felt like we needed to do everything we could to help him and that meant putting his needs ahead of ours.

We've tried to do that all along. We have a great relationship with him. He talks with us about being gay. If he has a date or whatever, he lets us know. We feel pretty good about where things are at right now.[26]

As you can see here, the tasks of seeking help and maintaining the relationship are intertwined. We've separated these tasks into two different chapters in order to unpack what each one entails, but the two are closely related.

YOUR TURN: MAINTAINING THE RELATIONSHIP

Take some time at the end of this chapter to reflect on a few questions related to the second task following disclosure: maintaining the relationship.

- What steps have you taken so far to maintain the relationship with your child?

- What additional steps are you considering?

- What did you think of the two pieces of advice from other Christian parents—to suspend judgment and to work on productive communication?

4

HOW THE PARENT-CHILD RELATIONSHIP CHANGES

Darlene and her husband, Mitch, have two boys, ages twenty-eight and twenty-six. The older boy, Michael, came out as gay to his parents when he was in college, about eight years ago. Their relationship with Michael prior to his coming out was "very good" and "close," according to Darlene and Mitch. They indicated that they talked a lot throughout Michael's childhood and adolescence. Michael was outgoing and highly involved at school. They described him as "easygoing" and "very likable," able to relate both to his peers and to adults in his teen years. Michael had a good sense of humor and was creative. Michael coming out as gay was a surprise to Darlene and Mitch. They were both initially shocked and had a mixture of feelings, including confusion, guilt, shame, fear, and anxiety. Their church's leaders believed not only that same-sex sexual behavior was morally impermissible, but also that gay people were sinning simply by experiencing same-sex attraction. This was not the official position of the church, but it was the message Darlene and Mitch heard when they shared with their cell group leader and a pastor that Michael was gay. These exchanges with church leaders informed how they as parents spoke to Michael, out of the assumption that his same-sex sexuality was willful disobedience. This perspective led to frequent arguments and a stony silence lasting nearly eighteen months. Missing the chance to connect with one another over the holidays and at birthdays and other events wore on Darlene and Mitch. Over time, they were able to listen to Michael and to ask better questions about his experience of same-sex sexuality and how he was making sense of his attractions. By then, Michael was wary of the Christian faith he was raised in. But he too wanted to re-connect, and he found that their willingness to ask better questions and listen to his answers seemed to offer them a fresh start, an opportunity to reconnect that was important to everyone.

In our last chapter we looked at the importance of maintaining the relationship with a child who has come out as gay. In this chapter we focus on how the parent-child relationship changes over time. We are eager to share this information with you because many parents find that it gives them hope to realize that things can improve, and hope can be good for everyone concerned.

> *Many parents find that it gives them hope to realize that things can improve.*

The parent-child relationship often, but not always, feels strained after disclosure. The nature of this strain can be far-ranging, including the emotional responses of both parents and child—some of which we have already discussed—but also including the quality of communication, the degree of relational authenticity, and other factors.

Campbell found that a fairly large percentage (41%) of parents reported a decrease in relationship quality at the time of their child's disclosure of same-sex sexuality compared to how they recall the relationship was prior to disclosure.[1] Parents rarely report any kind of immediate, positive change in their relationship at the time they found out their child was gay. But it is more common (51%) for parents to report that the quality of their relationship with their child stayed the same— that there was no real change in the relationship at the time of disclosure. If the relationship was already positive, it remained positive; if it was already negative, it remained negative.

The foundation parents have laid in their relationship with their children in years prior plays a significant role in the moment of disclosure. The strength and quality of the parent-child relationship is important to every major event in a child's life, and a child's coming out to their parents is a prime example of such an event. We want to see the parent-child relationship grow in depth and significance over time, encouraging parents and children to grow closer to one another if at all possible.

However, a good relationship prior to disclosure does not guarantee a continued good relationship after disclosure. Keep in mind that Campbell reports a decrease in relationship quality for a large percentage (41%) of parents, even if a higher percentage (51%) reported no such change.[2] What we want to explore in this chapter is how the parent-child relationship evolves over time. That is, now that disclosure has taken place and parents have (hopefully) made efforts to maintain the relationship, what happens to that relationship over the coming years (fig. 4.1)? Is it likely to improve? Get worse? Stay the same? What can we say about the relationship over time?

What we have seen is that, over time, positive relationships tend to continue to be positive, while relationships that initially suffered negative changes tend to improve over time. This is encouraging to know.

JEAN COLES ON HOW HER RELATIONSHIP WITH HER SON CHANGED

Our relationship was good and stayed good. At the same time, it's gotten deeper. We invited him to teach us when things we say or do are helpful or not helpful. We all kept the conversation open.

One of the things we learned from Greg is the importance of seeing him as a multifaceted individual, not simply as someone who is gay. He's an excellent communicator in multiple formats, including speaking, writing, songwriting, and musical performances. He's loving, compassionate, and wise beyond his years. He has excellent intuition, thinks carefully and deeply, and loves to learn. He's thoughtful and kind. He's a great worship leader. He's an amazing person, and we're so proud of him!

Where might parents expect improvements in their relationship over time, even if the relationship initially changed for the worse? Our research identified several areas of potential improvement, including increased emotional closeness, decreased conflict, improved communication, increased engagement or time spent together, increased authenticity, decreased anger, increased acceptance, and an increased sense of parental protectiveness or concern for their child.[3] Let's look at each of these dynamics as we organize them into two broad categories: (1) what may increase initially but decrease over time, and (2) what may decrease initially but increase over time.

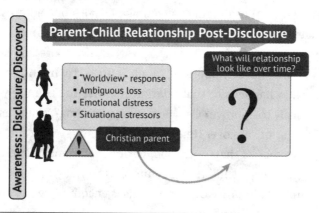

Figure 4.1. What will the parent-child relationship look like over time?

WHAT MAY INCREASE INITIALLY BUT TENDS TO DECREASE OVER TIME?

We first look at relational dynamics that may increase initially but tend to decrease over time. The two major dynamics parents report within this category are conflict and anger.[4]

Conflict. Not surprisingly, we often see an initial increase in parent-child conflict after a disclosure of same-sex sexuality. Darlene and Mitch, whom we introduced to you at the outset of this chapter, reported an increase in conflict with Michael at the time of disclosure. Their initial arguments ranged from theories of causation ("willful disobedience") to whether Michael was "really" gay because he had gone to prom with a girl. Darlene and Mitch didn't realize that Michael's limited dating history was intricately wound up with his same-sex sexuality: he had been exploring to see whether a heterosexual relationship would be possible for him, and also seeking to provide some cover for himself because he was not yet prepared to disclose his same-sex sexuality to his parents.

It is not uncommon to see an initial increase in parent-child relational conflict followed by a reduction in conflict over time. Keep in mind that if there is high conflict in the relationship prior to disclosure, there will likely also be conflict when parents learn that their child is gay, and that conflict may not naturally decrease. If the tools for negotiating conflict are not already in place prior to a child's coming out, the coming-out experience does not lend itself to providing these tools. But for most parents we interviewed, there was not significant conflict prior to the child's coming out, and when conflict was reported at the time of disclosure, that conflict tended to decrease over time.

For example, one parent described a specific conflict after their son's disclosure concerning "choice" and what aspects of his experience were volitional:

> We waited for an opportunity where [our son] was home by himself. We went downstairs, sat down and said, "We want to talk to you about this. We love you unconditionally. We don't care that you are gay." Then I said, "But if you're going to choose this. . . ." [Our son] flipped his head around at me and said, "I did not choose this! We do not choose being gay. I hate you. I don't want to talk to you about this." I lost it and started bawling. We tiptoed around each other for a while. We didn't really talk. It was the . . . elephant in the room.[5]

A mother shared about how conflict with her daughter increased significantly after she came out: "Oh my gosh. It was very tumultuous. I could never seem to say the right things. She was always angry at me. We were both hurt. She would say stuff to hurt me. Of course, I thought I was always right. We were just hurting each other. It was not good."

For another mother of a daughter who came out as gay, conflicts increased because of misunderstandings about the nature of the daughter's friendships and romantic interests: "Our relationship was really very strained. Suddenly, all of these things that she was doing with her girlfriends made me think [she] was dating like nine girls. I was like, 'Oh, you're going to dinner with this girl? But I thought you were dating this other girl? You're going to dinner with this other girl? What the hell!' I drove myself crazy thinking about it all the time."

A number of parents reported a kind of antagonism between themselves and their children—they gained awareness of how to push one another's buttons and then repeatedly chose to do so. Again, conflict and antagonism tend to decrease over time. It can be helpful to pace yourself, take the long view. Keep in mind that lashing out or responding to antagonism in kind has not been found to be helpful by other parents. Even though it may be an understandable response, it will not make things better.

Anger. The other experience that may increase initially after a child's disclosure but then tends to decrease over time is parental feelings of anger. This parental anger tends to be free-floating and may fall on different people. For Darlene and Mitch, the anger they reported was directed more toward God than toward Michael; most of their feelings toward Michael were feelings of confusion and guilt.

One mother shared about her anger toward God: "I felt that I was being tested. I had a rebellious attitude like, 'Oh, you are giving me this to deal with? Thanks, God.' I was angry that I was given this to deal with."[6]

> *"I felt that I was being tested. . . .*
> *I was angry that I was given this to deal with."*[7]

For other parents, anger might be directed toward their child and/or their child's same-sex partner. Here is an example of a mother's anger toward both her daughter and her daughter's partner shortly after learning her daughter was gay:

> There was a lot of anger towards this other woman [that my daughter was dating]. There was the anger of feeling like [my daughter] betrayed us, from all that we brought her up in through her years, that she would turn to this. [It was] a lot of emotional roller coaster, not knowing what to do or how to handle it. We couldn't even really stand to be around each other for a while.[7]

One mother shared of her anger toward her daughter, who had recently come out as lesbian: "I yelled and screamed. I said, 'How could you? You're going to go to hell.' I said terrible things. It was just such a shock to me. It was too much for me. It was so overwhelming. She was crying and I was crying. Basically, I was telling her what a horrible person she was and saying, 'How could you do this to me?'"[8]

Anger can sometimes function as a funnel emotion; that is, it can be the sole expressed emotion representing a whole variety of emotions experienced internally. What goes into the funnel is a wide range of feelings, but what comes out of the funnel is anger. In this mother's case, her self-preoccupation was probably tied to a variety of emotions she felt in response to her daughter's coming out. This self-preoccupation manifested in a kind of lashing out toward her daughter.

Another mother confessed her self-preoccupation more directly: "I was very self-centered in all of my thoughts. Looking back, I am ashamed. I was self-centered in that I had to be the one to deal with this, but I also wanted [my daughter] to be okay."[9]

In the months following her son's disclosure, one mother described her experience with a range of emotions directed toward her child, including anger: "I found myself questioning every move I made. I felt very guilty that I didn't realize [my son] was gay. I felt angry and confused that he could keep that from me, but mostly it was guilt that I missed that. [I thought], 'How did I miss that, and if I missed something that big, what else have I done wrong as a parent?'"[10]

Conflict and anger are two key experiences that, according to our research, often increase initially after disclosure but then decrease over time. We want to turn now to relational dynamics that tend to decrease initially but then increase over time (see fig. 4.2).

WHAT MAY DECREASE INITIALLY BUT TENDS TO INCREASE OVER TIME?

There may be several experiences that decrease initially but then tend to increase over time. These include emotional closeness, communication, engagement, authenticity, acceptance, and protectiveness. Let's look at each of these experiences.

Emotional closeness. Emotional closeness is a reflection of how close or distant a parent feels in relation to their LGBTQ+ child. It is common for parents to report an initial decrease in emotional closeness after disclosure, followed by an increase in emotional closeness over time. For Darlene and Mitch, there was an initial decrease in emotional closeness with Michael as they tried to figure out what was going on. They turned to others for support and guidance, receiving some unhelpful suggestions that only exacerbated the distance they felt. This distance lasted for months before they began to see improvement in their sense of closeness with Michael.

A mother shared with us her experience of decreased emotional closeness at the time her son disclosed his same-sex sexuality to her. There were many complicating circumstances that made the disclosure more challenging:

> That was the worst my relationship had ever been with [my son] as a mom. I knew he was lying. I knew that things were not adding up. You know in your gut as a mom when he says he's somewhere and he's not. We just knew it. This kid that never lied in his life . . . was lying, so our relationship started drifting further and further apart. This kid who was very demonstrative and touchy feely started pushing away from everyone, even his sister who he's extremely close to now. During that phase it was as if he was trying to get away. [It was] very, very difficult.[11]

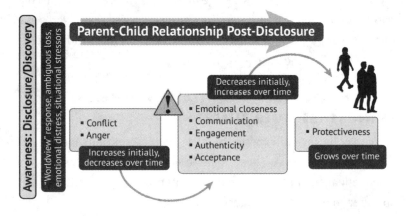

Figure 4.2. Changes in parent-child relationship post-disclosure

It is important to note that this mother described her season of decreased emotional closeness with her son as a phase, not something sustained over time. Initial loss of closeness doesn't mean the relationship cannot improve over time.

We see a similar loss of closeness in another mother's experience:

I think there has been a distancing, which is very sad. God has been working on me, giving me love, and helping me come to grips with this, but it has not been reciprocal [from my daughter]. I don't know why. We have not had that conversation with her. For us, our faith is drawing us to her, but for her I think our faith is a distancing factor. There is this gap. . . . I think she was very hurt that her dad would not marry her as a pastor. She probably feels some type of emotional alienation.[12]

Unfortunately, there is no guarantee that every parent-child relationship will grow in emotional closeness over time. However, this is a common experience, even in cases where an initial decrease in emotional closeness at the time of disclosure makes it difficult to imagine the restoration of former closeness.

One mother described how her sense of emotional closeness with her son has increased over time since his disclosure: "He seems closer to me. He finds things online—scientific things about how people are gay—and he will share those things with me. He's learning along the way that I'm learning. It brought us closer as a mother and a son."[13]

Another parent shared, "It has given us a lot more topics to discuss, even silly things like I just watched this funny video on how to be gay. We can laugh about that stuff together."[14]

Another parent describes their relationship with their child coming full circle, returning to how things were before their world was upended by their child's disclosure. Stories like this one may give some parents hope:

[Our relationship is] back to where it was before. Lots of communication. I think he feels very loved and accepted and [knows that he can] come to us with concerns and problems. He's closer now to his dad than he ever has been. Looking back, we see that there was that phase with his dad, where his dad would be so disappointed in him in the past. Now he understands how proud his dad is of him. So, on a scale of 1 to 10 it's a 20. It's great. Our family is as close as it's ever been.[15]

Of course, increased closeness does not happen by accident. Houp found that parent contact with other people who were gay had a significant influence on parents' closeness with their child.[16] This contact often came via their child's friendships or as parents took part in their child's interests, events, and activities, as well as through contact in the parent's own communities (for example, their place of employment and place of worship). Other avenues to regaining closeness include, again, pacing yourself and your relationship with your child, giving yourself time, and finding areas of shared interest, some of which may have been present but were discontinued, such as gardening, cooking together, shopping. Such activities could now be resumed, not with a focus on discussing sexuality or gender but to just be together with one another in satisfying areas of mutual interest.

Communication. Improved communication can be measured both by the quality or authenticity of communication and by the frequency of communication. Our research generally dealt with the frequency of communication, although we also noted improvements in the quality of communication. For Darlene and Mitch, both the quality and the frequency of communication with Michael dropped precipitously after his disclosure. This reduced communication seemed to be closely tied to their conflict about Michael's "willful disobedience," as well as Darlene and Mitch's initial understanding of what Michael was saying and how he had reached his conclusions.

As we have noted, communication can initially decrease significantly after a child's coming out. We see this dynamic in one parent's description: "You didn't see her much. She kind of stayed away. When she was here, it was very hard for my husband and I. We did not know how to handle it and it was very hard. I would say that it was easier for us to almost want to ignore it and ignore her, because it hurt so bad."[17]

A mother shared her own experience of decreased communication with her son:

[My son] was distant. Up to that point, I had always been able to ask [him] questions. Whether he wanted to fully answer them was another matter, but I thought that I could continue doing that. I wanted to understand more about where he was and what he was doing and thinking. [I was] really trying to get a grip on how to define this. Even though I'm very artistic, I'm very analytical as well, and if I can pick something apart, I feel better. Whether I have all the answers or not, lay this out on the table for me. Let me see all the parts. He didn't want to do that. He got angry. There were moments of seeing my son and having good moments of conversation, but they were so few.[18]

We see a similar decrease in communication described by this mother after her daughter came out, followed by an increase in communication after the mother's request that they talk:

One time she told me, "I just don't want to talk about this, Mom." We had had a conversation that was really good about just talking about it. I said, "I have to process with you . . . even if you don't like talking about it. I need you to talk with me because that's how I am. I know you just want to say it and move on. You don't want to have these conversations, but they're really important." Thankfully she honored that plea from me to talk with me about it. I think that was really helpful. I think it was helpful for both of us because even though she doesn't like to talk, I really feel like it opened a door to more authentic communication in general than we had ever had. We would always talk, but this opened an opportunity to have more meaningful, authentic conversations, and I'm really glad about that.[19]

Another mother noted an increase in communication with her son since his initial disclosure: "It is just a lot better. . . . He says 'I love you' now. He wrote on Facebook one day, 'I love my mom.' He is still not close with my husband. With me we are close and open. He is talking to me about teenage issues, politics, religion, sexuality, me being a teenager, every-thing. We have very good conversations. He hugs me, everything."[20]

Engagement. Engagement has to do with how much time a parent spends with their child who came out to them. Just like communication, engagement often drops after a child comes out; however, some parents are very intentional about leaning into their relationship with their child after disclosure. One parent recalled, "I think I felt more of a need to be with him to try to understand it. I didn't want to be locked out of his world."[21]

That desire to stay connected, to not be locked out of their son's world, was also true for Darlene and Mitch as they described their relationship with Michael. Still, like many parents, they faced great anguish and be-wilderment as they struggled to find a pathway to healthy engagement with their child. Engaging with a child who discloses same-sex sexuality can initially be painful for parents. It can be fraught. People can speak past one another, and many will simply not engage for a season as they try to understand what they should do and how to move forward.

One father shared with us some of what his relationship with his son was like before the son came out as gay:

> My relationship with him was always one of love, care, concern, and support. [It was a] typical father/son relationship. I supported him in his activities, both academic, extracurricular, and church. I tried to be as involved and supportive as I could be and yet foster independence [in him in order] to grow him up and release him. I did things with him and liked to be involved with his activities to the best of my ability and to his ability to allow me to do that.[22]

This father's engagement with his son was a reflection of the love and care he felt, evidenced by time spent together in various activities. Un-fortunately, forms of engagement that sometimes feel uncomplicated to parents prior to disclosure can sometimes become complicated by the knowledge of a child's same-sex sexuality.

Another father described what he experienced as higher engagement with his son prior to disclosure:

We homeschooled our kids through their elementary years, so we spent a lot of time with [our son] in that way. [My wife] did a lot of that, but then I also did quite a bit by the time he was in fourth or fifth grade. I have been in pastoral ministry all my life, so I had a little bit of flexibility to spend some middle-of-the-day hours with the kids. [My son] was always very inquisitive and bright. I felt like I had a positive relationship with him. We did a lot of stuff together as a family. By the time he was a sophomore in high school, he was the only child at home, so we followed his music and sports and extracurricular-type activities. Between [my wife and me], we were almost always at one of them. Sometimes we were there together.[23]

For many parents, the parent-child relationship immediately following disclosure was characterized by a sudden decrease in engagement. Fortunately, parents who report this decrease in engagement often find that it eventually gives way to an increase in engagement over time. Things that other parents say helped included understanding the topic a little better, recognizing that this is not a phase for their child but an ongoing experience or enduring reality, getting some of the spiritual questions they had answered, finding that some of the fears they had initially lessened over time, and so on.

Authenticity. Authenticity refers to both the parent and the child being able to "be themselves" with one another.[24] Authentic relationships have a sense of honesty and openness. Children in an authentic relationship with their parents might say that they are able to bring all of themselves to the relationship.

> *Authentic relationships have a sense of honesty and openness.*

This desire to be authentic, and to make room for their child to be authentic, was certainly voiced by both Darlene and Mitch. They did not want Michael to pretend to be someone he was not. However, they had to navigate many questions and beliefs surrounding causation, volition, and the meaning of same-sex attractions. Their approach to these questions sometimes made it difficult for them to be authentic with Michael or give him freedom to be authentic with them.

As with communication, authenticity can often decrease initially after disclosure but then improve over time. For example, one parent described decreased authenticity: "It was strained, but I think she could see that I was trying. She certainly got more support from me than her dad. She tried to talk to me a few times about it early on, and I wasn't ready. She would make funny little gay jokes. She's hilarious, but I wasn't ready for that. I think humor was her way of trying to break the ice and bridge the gap between us."[25]

Another parent described an increase in authenticity in how he experienced his relationship with his son over time, from first learning his son was gay to several years later when he was interviewed:

> It hasn't changed a lot, other than over the last eight years, it's gotten much more supportive. I would say it [our son's sexuality] doesn't matter anymore. I can't come up with the words, but over these eight years, it's evolved from being guarded the first couple of years and not wanting to talk a lot about it, to talking more about it, to it's just part of the everyday conversation.[26]

There are many ways to grow in authenticity, and these ways can be value-congruent for you as a parent and for your child. Parents and children may face greater challenges when they have different values on important topics, but there remain many ways to be close to and authentic with one another despite important differences of belief or conviction.

LYNN AND GREG McDONALD ON HOW THEIR RELATIONSHIP WITH THEIR SON CHANGED OVER TIME

It took a couple of years of not having a close relationship with Greg Jr. before things got worse and changed. Greg Jr. had multiple conversations with his dad about me (Lynn) and how I kept beating him and his friends with the Bible. He said if it continued, he would not visit us again. Whoa! That was not what I wanted to happen. What was I doing wrong that my son would not want to be with me?

His words challenged me to seek deep within myself. I spent a lot of time asking Jesus to open my eyes to what I was doing wrong. I decided to turn the situation around. If Greg Jr. was treating my friends and me the way I was his, would I want to spend time with him? The answer was definitely not. I realized I made them my project, and making someone a project never ends well; that had to stop. I apologized to Greg Jr., and he forgave me, but moving forward, he still was unsure if I would be safe.

With Lynn and I (Greg) trying to fix or change Greg Jr., we had become unsafe. When Greg Jr. and his friends stopped coming around, it became painfully clear that we had lost voice or influence with the very son I would give my life for. We became determined to love him and his friends just the way they were, unconditionally, the same way Jesus loves all of us. That proved to be a very wise decision. At some point, Lynn and I both apologized to Greg Jr. for trying to fix him. We explained that, in hindsight, we could see that our words and actions were very hurtful. Greg Jr. was very gracious as always and accepted our sincere apologies.

Nonetheless, he kept us at arm's length for several months until he saw our actions matched our words. Eventually, he and his friends began visiting us again. As time went on, we not only grew closer to our son and his friends, but Greg Jr.'s relationship with Jesus really blossomed. What greater gift could a parent have than to see their child grow closer to Jesus?

Our change in behavior was so attractive that one of Greg Jr.'s college friends asked us if we would consider being his adopted mom and dad, as his Christian family had kicked him out of the house and disowned him. This was the first in a long line of adult LGBTQ individuals who asked that we adopt them as well. Over time we affectionately became known as "McMom and McDad."

A critical learning we discovered along the way is that if a parent isn't safe with their child, they will not be trusted. If they are not trusted, they will not have a meaningful relationship. If there is no relationship, they will not have any influence. This same formula is true for any relationship. Safety is paramount!

Acceptance. *Acceptance* can be a tricky word. For some parents, acceptance means coming to terms with the reality of a situation. That is how we use the word. For other parents, acceptance can mean giving up or accepting defeat. Still other parents might think of acceptance as an affirmational stance that they feel conflicted about because of their Christian commitments.

For Darlene and Mitch, acceptance meant coming to terms with reality. In other words, they eventually came to a point where they acknowledged the reality of Michael's same-sex sexuality. They realized that it was not something Michael had chosen, that it was part of his experience, and that he would face choices related to his sexuality in the months and years ahead.

Other parents have had different experiences of acceptance. Here is an example of a parent whose beliefs and values changed over time toward a theological view that affirms same-sex marriage:

> It's so much better for us, being able to whole-heartedly [give approval]. The unfortunate thing is my son is not at the same place spiritually as I'd like him to be, and I don't know that he'll ever be at that place, because his faith and views have been altered by experience. But at least I know now that I could say it differently to a child now. I could give approval, and they don't even need to ask me for it. I don't have that angst. But as a parent, you love your child, and it's so much about what you're coming out of and who's influencing you at the time.[27]

The parents we meet with often find it helpful to distinguish between their love of their child, their acceptance of the reality of their child's same-sex sexuality, and their beliefs or values about whether same-sex sexual behavior is morally permissible.

For some parents, acceptance of their child felt impossible unless it was accompanied by a belief in the permissibility of same-sex sexual relationships. One mother explains her conviction as a way of affirming what Houp calls "the entirety of her child":[28]

> If Jesus was here today, He would be on the side of the gay person, who is being persecuted. He wouldn't be against them. It's all about

love, and we are supposed to love one another. That starts with God, and it goes immediately to our children. Love your child. You can't do the whole, "Love the sinner, hate the sin." Being gay is who [my son] is. It's his fabric. If I hate the sin of him being gay, then I hate him. Love your child first and foremost.[29]

In contrast to this example of a more gay-affirming acceptance, some parents reported increased acceptance in the sense of supporting their child relationally while continuing to object to the child's sexual orientation or behavior. For example, one father remembers separating relational support and theological support in his relationship with his daughter:

The next day we sat down and I opened up the scripture and explained how I see this. I pointed out that there are a lot of things that can cause someone to not inherit the kingdom of God and that this was one of them. She handled that well. Then I said, "I hope we can just process this, and I hope we can have a better relationship." I wanted to reach out as a father, not even considering the same-sex attraction. . . . [My daughter] said, "That would be good, but I don't want you to feel like you have to fix me, Dad. You're not going to fix me." So that explained where she was at. That's how I viewed it at that point for sure.[30]

For many Christian parents, acceptance is connected to their beliefs and values in complex ways. Here is an example of a parent grappling with unconditional love for her son while not approving of her son's sexual orientation.

He wanted approval . . . and I, at that time, could not give approval. I kept saying, "It's God's to give," and I didn't know what to do with it. He was very patient, but we had some doozy fights over that and religion. So, it did become quite heated and I could say that I loved him unconditionally, but for him to really not feel like there was still some condition being held out. And I didn't have it yet . . . nor did my husband.[31]

Another parent shared how they had found it helpful to distinguish between sexual orientation and sexual activity, understanding the unchosen nature of same-sex sexuality while continuing to believe in the importance of choices about sexual behavior:

> For me, I just have to believe [my son's sexual orientation is] not a choice. I feel it was how he was created. I think what he does with it is the choice, that's what I've come to believe. If he chose to be celibate, God would be there for him. That's it in a nutshell. I would like him to choose to let God totally be the center of his life and for him to find his strength, worth, and whatever he needs from his relationship with God.[32]

We will return in chapter five to the topic of acceptance in relation to theological beliefs and decisions about church membership, but already we can begin to see how Christian parents' navigation of the parent-child relationship post-disclosure is often tied to their religious beliefs and values.

HOW THE RELATIONSHIP CHANGES WITH TRANSGENDER CHILDREN

Like parents of same-sex-oriented children, parents of transgender children tend to report initial increases in anger and conflict, followed by decreases over time. They also report initial decreases, followed by increases over time, in closeness, communication, engagement, authenticity, and acceptance. However, the journey for Christian parents of transgender children is also unique in some ways. Because exploration of gender identity can include the possibility of a partial or complete gender transition, these parents will often share that they feel they are losing their son or daughter. As a result, they face real grief. Parents should not use this grief as a means of manipulating their child, nor should they wield their grief as a weapon against their child, as though the child were responsible for it. Transgender children are trying to navigate their gender dysphoria, and we want parents to be a resource to them throughout that journey. By fostering healthy relationship with their transgender child, Christian parents will be better situated to encourage their child's relationship with God, helping them find ways to manage their distress and grow in their faith.

Parents are often encouraged to know that parental relationships with a child navigating gender identity tend to improve over time. Of course, this improvement may come along multiple different pathways. Some children may decide to cope with their gender dysphoria without transitioning, which others pursue social or medical transition. In each case, the kind of relational improvement parents experience may look different. For example, one mother of a transgender daughter (a child who is biologically male but experiences their self as a girl) shared how the closeness she felt with her child existed before her child came out as transgender and continued after her child's disclosure:

> [My transgender daughter] and I were very, very close. I worked full time and we lived together. It was just a very good upbringing. We were very close [pre-disclosure]. . . . My feelings towards [her] never changed [post-disclosure] as far as me loving her. If you were to ask me now about my daughter, I think that my daughter has more courage than anybody that I know. That's how I would describe my daughter.[a]

Some parents might find this quote challenging to read. You may not feel willing to accept his kind of path. In our experience, you will need time and support to name and work through the grief and other emotions you may experience as you reengage in relationship with your child. Your child needs you as they weigh decisions about living with enduring dysphoria or departing from expected gender presentations. You do not have to affirm every decision your child may make (or has already made), but they do need to know you love them and will continue to walk with them.

WHAT TENDS TO GROW OVER TIME?

We also saw an increase in parental protectiveness toward their child over time. Increased protectiveness did not follow the same pattern as other increases such as communication and acceptance, which tended to decrease initially before increasing over time. Rather, protectiveness tended to develop over time for some parents without any initial decrease. Initially, the protectiveness parents felt was sometimes motivated by their fears. But while fear for the future and increased protectiveness of a child may be related, they are somewhat different in our experience.

Darlene and Mitch eventually discussed with us some of the protectiveness they felt for Michael. Their protectiveness was primarily motivated not by concern for Michael's physical safety but by their uncertainty about what it could look like for Michael to be in emotionally and spiritually safe spaces. This included concern about finding a local faith community where he would be welcomed, in light of some of the beliefs and assumptions they encountered when they were first seeking help and resources from their church community. As time went on, they had a better sense of what Michael would face in a church like the one he grew up in.

Protectiveness often takes the form of concern for a child's emotional safety or spiritual well-being, as it did in Darlene and Mitch's case. For example, parents may be concerned that their child will have to deal with future discrimination due to their sexual orientation, whether in social settings, in employment or housing, or at their place of worship. In other cases, parents' protectiveness may be driven by concerns about their child's physical safety, as in situations of anti-gay bullying or prejudicially motivated violence.

One parent described her fears as being tied not only to external factors but even more to her son's internal struggle; she worried about his well-being and self-perception in the midst of his own coming to terms with himself:

> Mostly there was an anxiety about him being comfortable with himself. [I wanted him] to stop tormenting himself and stop thinking he can change it. I was worried that he would make himself nutty if he continued to try to be something that he wasn't. It was the kind of anxiety that you would have for your child,

because you want them to be happy with who they are and what they are, and safe. Safety is one thing that always comes to mind. It would just crush me if somebody were to hurt him or if he were to not be able to get a job because someone suspected he was gay or something like that.[33]

The main change that appears to take place for parents is a shift over time from being consumed by their fears for their child—which is more of an anxiety-based response at or shortly following disclosure—to a kind of protectiveness on behalf of their child that develops over time. This shift is independent of the parents' theological views, as most of our parent were more traditional in their views, as we will discuss in chapter five. This protectiveness can be a healthy way to take charge of one's fears in practical ways. These may include ongoing discussions with their child that don't put their child on the spot but reflect increased awareness of the challenges their child may face, safety planning, and even value-congruent advocacy in certain spaces, such as church or small group ministry.

THE CONTACT HYPOTHESIS

Contact with people who are LGBTQ+ helped some of our Christian parents improve their relationship with their child. These relational improvements seem to represent a specific example of the "contact hypothesis," the view that having contact with others from a different group can reduce prejudice toward that group.[34] In our research, we found that contact with LGBTQ+ people tended to alleviate some of the relational difficulties Christian parents faced after a child's disclosure of same-sex sexuality.

> *Having contact with others from a different group can reduce prejudice toward that group.*

When we say that contact with LGBTQ+ people reduced parental prejudice, we are not necessarily implying that beliefs about the sinfulness of same-sex sexual behavior are always rooted in prejudice or that these beliefs disappeared as prejudice disappeared. Parents' beliefs about sexual ethics may well be thoughtful judgments that remain consistent over time. But the contact hypothesis seemed to illuminate relational dynamics far beyond theological questions about sexual behavior. To examine these dynamics, we studied parents' contact with extended family members who were gay and with the gay community more broadly. Parents' contact with LGBTQ+ people also sometimes took place through their child's life, events, or activities, or through friendships that a child or parent had at their workplace or in their local faith community.

With whom do Christian parents report having the most contact? For the Christian parents we interviewed, gay family members were their most frequent point of contact with a member of the gay community.[35] However, parents' chosen friendships with gay people were typically a better indicator of their prejudices and attitudes toward homosexuality, whereas unchosen family relationships with gay people were less directly indicative of parents' attitudes. We saw glimpses of this dynamic in a separate study in which gay Christians whose parents had experiences or friendships with people in the gay community reported better experiences coming out to their parents.[36] According to a related finding from Houp, parent contact with the gay community had a significant influence on the parent's own closeness with their gay child.[37]

Houp reported that the most common LGBTQ+ point of contact for Christian parents was a family member.[38] The parent of one LGBTQ+ child wrote,

> My sister is LGBT. . . . She's my sister, she's our family, and she's still the same person. We didn't approve of what she was doing at the time, but that wasn't going to stop us from visiting her or hanging out with her. That was what we told our kids when my sister came out. We said, "We're still going to love [your aunt] even though she is now separated from her husband and has moved in with this girl. She's still your aunt. We're going to love her." So at least I had that much to go by. I had worked through that part.[39]

One parent described her relationships with gay coworkers, attributing the contact with those coworkers to God's provision for her in the present moment:

> I believe God put my coworkers in my life to prepare me [for my son's disclosure]. I'm so glad I had them and that they trusted me enough with their stories. Because a couple of them were just very mistreated. It just breaks me up now thinking about it. One fellow was literally thrown out of his home. He was 14 years old and on the street. What do you do? He was taken advantage of. It was just an incredible story. I know looking back that God put those people in my life so that I would be prepared, but I never allowed myself to go there.[40]

Another mother described how her friendships with LGBTQ+ people influenced her view that gay people were also God's children. This conviction became meaningful to her in navigating her relationship with her child:

> I had some friends who were homosexual online. [My view of homosexuality] just didn't really come up, we didn't discuss that. I knew they were gay, but it didn't draw me away from them. I looked at it as wrong but not as I wanted to stay away from them. It was not something so terrible that I couldn't be around them. I looked at it more as that they were still God's children.[41]

Contact through a child's friends, including the child's romantic partners, can be tricky. One parent's response captures the challenge they feel in getting to know the people who matter to their son while continuing to disagree with homosexuality generally: "We have met his gay boyfriend. We have had him at our house. We have done things with him. If that's going to be his life and I love him, then I have to love that part of him as well. I still don't like it. I still wish it would go away."[42]

Contact with members of the gay community does not mean that a parent's worldview will abruptly or completely shift. But contact may thicken the plot as to who gay people are, causing parents to realize that gay people don't all believe the same things or behave the same way. In other words, gay people are a heterogeneous group; there is no one experience of being gay. As we have seen, contact with gay people can occur through many avenues of relationship.

ADVICE FROM CHRISTIAN PARENTS

Keep as many doors open as possible. One piece of advice offered by Christian parents with gay kids to others in similar situations is to keep as many doors as possible open to the relationship. In other words, maintain and invest in every possible avenue for future relationship. These should not be conditional doors; rather, keep open every door you can possibly keep open. This may be especially hard if your child is choosing to maintain their distance from you, as one parent described: "I think there has been a distancing, which is very sad. God has been working on me, giving me love, and helping me come to grips with this, but it has not been reciprocal [from my daughter]."[43]

> *Doors should not be conditional.*
> *Keep open every door you can possibly keep open.*

While it can be discouraging for parents to continue to hold relational doors open when their children choose relational distance, this distance is sometimes a season in the child's life that will ultimately give way to a new season of relational openness. Children may believe that they need temporary space so they can be in a better position to have a relationship later on. We advise you to give your child the space they request while keeping as many doors open to the relationship as you are able.

Stay focused on the most important things. Most parents we have worked with come to see us with concerns about their child's sexuality after their child comes out to them as gay. However, if their child later distances themselves from Christianity or rejects the faith they were raised in, parents become more concerned about that, and concerns about their child's sexuality diminish. It is as though parents recognize a hierarchy of concerns, and they conclude that helping their child nurture a struggling faith or regain a lost faith is their highest priority.

This shifting of priorities can also affect the parent-child relationship over time. Many adult children revisit the faith they were raised in; they may be in a different place spiritually as they enter late adolescence or young adulthood.

We are not suggesting that a focus on relational priorities should lead parents to leave their church or to abandon their beliefs and values. We will examine in chapter five the ways in which parents' experience of faith changes over time. However, we have seen time and time again that parents' concerns about their child's sexual orientation tend to diminish as they become more eager to foster the faith journey of their child, making sure that their child knows God loves them and wants to draw them closer to him.

YOUR TURN: HOW THE PARENT-CHILD RELATIONSHIP CHANGES OVER TIME

Take some time at the end of this chapter to reflect on a few questions related to how parent-child relationships tend to change over time:

- Many parents note an initial increase in conflict and free-floating anger after a child's disclosure of same-sex sexuality, but this conflict and anger also tend to decrease over time. What has your experience been like so far?

- Many parents note an initial decrease in relational features such as communication, closeness, and authenticity after a child's disclosure of same-sex sexuality, but a subsequent increase in these areas over time. What has your experience been like so far?

- What do you think about the two closing pieces of advice offered by Christian parents to one another: (1) keep as many doors as possible open to a relationship and (2) stay focused on the most important things? What questions do you have about the best ways to do these things?

5

HOW FAITH CHANGES

Darnell and Deja came in for counseling after their daughter, Asia, age seventeen, had come out to them as gay. Both Darnell and Deja stated that they believed the Bible taught that homosexuality was a sin. More specifically, they viewed same-sex relationships and sexual behavior as sinful; they had not given much thought to whether same-sex attractions themselves were sinful, but they seemed to lean toward viewing such attractions as "not good," since they saw attractions as leading to behavior. In the course of our counseling together, they also shared their questions about why God allowed some people to experience same-sex attractions and whether God made people gay; although they did not hold this latter view when they initiated counseling, their daughter's experience had made them less certain. They struggled, too, over whether to share with their pastor about their journey with Asia. They respected their pastor, but they felt he had been outspoken in the past about homosexuality in ways that made them doubt whether he would be able to be much of a resource now to them or to Asia.

Like Darnell and Deja, most Christian parents we have interviewed shared that, prior to their child's coming out, they held the belief that homosexuality (either same-sex behavior or same-sex attraction) was sin.[1] However, many of these parents came to question this belief over time. Still other parents never viewed homosexuality as a sin, even prior to their child's coming out. As we will see below, Christian parents tend to stay in their local church after a child comes out to them. Parents who stay in their church may find it helpful to identify a handful of people with whom they can be honest about what they believe and the questions they are asking about their beliefs. These friends who join parents on their journey should be the kind of people with whom parents experience emotional and spiritual safety. They are not going to say or do things that would feel threatening at a time of great vulnerability.

Before we look at specific beliefs about sexual behavior and decisions parents face about whether to remain in their current church, we want to look at Christian parents' broader spiritual journey. We include in this discussion of spiritual journey experiences with prayer, reading Scripture, trust in God, and their faith community (see fig. 5.1).

CHRISTIAN PARENTS' SPIRITUAL JOURNEY

How Christian parents reflect on their own beliefs and values—which we consider in greater detail below—seems to be related to their spiritual journey, particularly the ways they make meaning out of a difficult situation as they attempt to discern God's purposes in their lives and in the lives of their children.

Many parents resonated with this theme. Not all the parents experienced a strengthening of their faith, but most did.[2] They often said that God had expanded their capacity for faith or trust in him by being present with them through what seemed like an impossible set of circumstances. The idea of dependency on God during a difficult time was common, as one parent's comments demonstrate: "You depend on God so much in these times and you are digging deeper in your faith. You don't have it all figured out. You're trying to figure it out, but you're in this place of total dependency on Him to get you through. It takes a lot of prayer."[3]

It was not uncommon for parents to emphasize the importance of their child's relationship with God rather than focusing narrowly on their child's sexuality. These parents focused on facilitating their child's walk with God whenever possible.

We also know that some parents avoided asking certain difficult spiritual questions because they were concerned about the answers they might find, as Houp suggests.[4] One parent in our most recent survey said, "I keep believing how I've always believed but continue to pray like I'm wrong."[5]

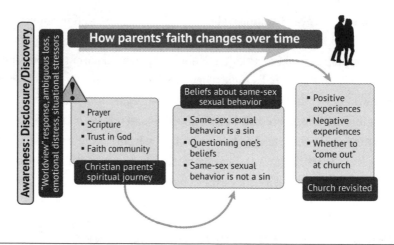

Figure 5.1. How parents' faith changes over time

If you are a parent who is questioning God, struggling with God, or bewildered by what God is doing in this moment, you are not alone. Many Christian parents have reported similar experiences. If you are a parent who is questioning God, you are not alone.

If your experience is like the experiences of the Christian parents we interviewed, you might be feeling strong negative emotions, such as anger, toward God. Here is a parent's honest appraisal of their anger toward God after their son came out:

> At first, I was angry at God, because I thought, "Lord, what else do you expect me to go through? I don't think I can handle this. I don't think I can go through this on top of everything else." I felt so devastated and angry with God that he would do that. At the same time, even in my anger I still trusted the Lord to take me through it. I usually run to the Word and to the Lord when I'm hurting, even though I may be angry with him or don't understand. . . . So, I just kept working through it, praying, and asking the Lord that maybe there would be a change [in my son]. As I have become more and more educated, I know it is in God's hands. There are a lot of ways that God handles this with different people.[6]

It is okay to experience anger and to bring that anger to God and name it. You might be wondering whether God made your child this way and, if so, what that means for your beliefs about homosexuality and whether same-sex behavior or same-sex orientation is sinful. It is okay to ask these questions and to bring them to God for direction. You might be asking more broadly how God in his sovereignty could allow this to happen, given how painful it is for you as a parent, for your child, or for the relational strain that may now exist. Again, it is okay to wrestle honestly with these profound questions. These questions make sense to us and to many parents who have faced similar circumstances.

Deepening prayer. Mother Teresa once shared, "God speaks in the silence of the heart, and we listen. And then we speak to God from the fullness of our heart, and God listens. And this listening and this speaking is what prayer is meant to be."[7] Indeed, prayer was an important source of comfort and support for many of the Christian parents we interviewed. One father captures this dynamic well:

> My faith has probably gotten stronger, believe it or not. [Faith] was something that I've relied on in the past through trying situations, deaths, major issues and things that have come up in my life. Again, I turned to that to the best of my extent and prayed. I hear lots of people talking about prayer and what it is and what it's not. I think prayer needs to be as much if not more listening than a conversation, so I have got to shut up and listen. I did some prayer and I said, "I don't have the answers to this, let me just listen to you, God, and seek direction in this." It has really helped me mature in my faith walk in a phenomenal way.[8]

Another parent shared how prayer became a key avenue for them to experience God's guidance throughout the journey—a more reliable source of information than the differing opinions of people on either side of debates about Christianity and sexuality: "Also, the biggest, biggest piece is look to God through prayer. People will tell you all sorts of things from both sides, but let God guide you. That's going to take a lot of laying down yourself to be able to listen. I'm still not completely there. Our life is day by day and it's not just [our son], it's everything that the world throws at us."⁹

Many Christian parents referenced prayer as part of their spiritual journey post-disclosure. They often portrayed prayer as a Christ-follower's personal conversation with God, emphasizing the importance of listening and being attuned to what God is saying.

Immersed in Scripture. It was not uncommon for Christian parents to spend time in Scripture. For some, reading the Bible was a spiritual discipline that, along with prayer and corporate worship, served as a lifeline during a tumultuous season in their lives.

Other parents turned to Scripture to revisit the ways they previously understood certain texts, especially on matters of sexuality, sexual orientation, and sexual behavior. One mother shared what it meant to her to challenge her previously held interpretations in the hope that those interpretations were flawed.

Another parent advised fellow parents to reconsider the true nature of sin in Scripture:

> Really examine what the biblical perspective is on sin. Really know what God thinks about sin and what Jesus taught about sin and who He had his company with. Jesus was not always hanging out with the godly people. He was trying to make relationships with people who had sin issues in their lives. He even pointed out all the sin that everybody has. You think you're living this perfect life and it's just a lie. Get over it and bring the sinners to God. Don't be shunning people and being judgmental.¹⁰

One mother described a shift in her interpretation of Scripture between the time her child came out and the time of the interview:

> As far as scriptures that relate with same-sex [sexuality], in the past I would have been closed-minded; that's what it says. I had a very judgmental, harsh, unloving approach. Now where we're at is: Yes, we love God's word. We know what it says, but man is flawed some- times in our understanding of how it's lived out. So, we are willing

to live in tension, knowing that we don't have a complete under-standing and all of us fall short of the glory of God.[11]

Though this mother hasn't totally overturned her prior beliefs, she has softened in her wielding of Scripture in relation to others. She argues for humility in determining how the truths of the Scriptures are to be lived out in relationships.

Trust in God. Trust in God often has to do with our beliefs about God's provision and God's sovereignty over our circumstances, including the challenges we are facing. One parent described his trust in God and in God's ability to care for his daughter's future shortly after she came out to him as gay:

> We had some great milestone faith moments together, so even though I really did not understand and it's painful as a parent, in those moments, I chose to trust God with her. I don't know where I got this phrase—maybe [I] read it—but I started reminding myself that this is not the end of this story. It was just where we were right then I had to keep reminding myself that God has a great future in store for her. I had to keep immersing myself in trusting God with [my daughter]. [My daughter] chose Christ at a young age. She was baptized. This was not the whole story; this was just a part of the story.[12]

Trust in God is often most necessary in areas of great importance to parents, such as their child's salvation. Shortly after her daughter came out as gay, a mother stressed the importance of trusting God with her daughter's walk with him:

> My marriage of twenty-five years is falling apart because I have been supportive of my daughter and chosen to love her and to not care who she's with. I'd rather have a gay Christian daughter than an unsaved straight one. I know she's saved. I hope at one point she'll be comfortable to come back to church, but she got so hurt at our church that I think it's going to take a long time for that to happen.[13]

Another parent described the powerlessness that drove them to rely on
God more completely: "You are powerless unless you become like a child.
I now understand that means that a child is completely dependent on its
father. I did not grasp that before. I just thought it meant that you had
to be innocent, but it means to completely turn over all of this to him.
Tell him, 'I trust you with it, in your time, not mine.'"[14]

A mother of a gay son shared something similar about her growth
in trust:

> I started to trust that God knows what He's doing and that the most
> important thing for my son is for him to have the Holy Spirit in his
> life. Once he has that, then the Holy Spirit will guide him in what's
> right or wrong. I, as his mom, don't have to find all the answers,
> and I can just be okay with who he is and where he is. I don't have
> to put a label on it, good or bad. I didn't need to do that. I started
> to feel comfortable with those sorts of feelings for myself. I felt at
> peace with it through my prayer and reading.[15]

The Christian parents we interviewed frequently mentioned that
learning to trust God was an aspect of their spiritual journey that
expanded in capacity over time after their child came out.

Part of a faith community. Many parents also discussed the importance of their participation (or a change of their participation status) in
a local faith community. We will further unpack parents' connection to
faith community in the next section, but for now we want to acknowledge the role of faith communities in many parents' lives. One
mother shared with us how her church participation changed in the
weeks and months following her daughter's disclosure: "I continued to
go to church. [My daughter] and I found another church together that
we went to. It is a really good church that I still attend. I couldn't wait
to go; I was excited about going to church for the first time in a long
time. I joined a Bible study and I asked everybody that I knew to pray
for me and for my daughter."[16]

Some parents, such as this mother, had good experiences in faith
communities—whether the same community they had been part of

prior to their child's coming or a new community. Others reported bad experiences in faith communities. Parents' experiences in Christian institutions such as churches were often interpersonally mediated, meaning that their relationships with others could make or break a parent's experience. Some of the challenges parents encountered in their churches were related to the church's doctrinal positions. For many Christian parents, however, the primary challenges they encountered had more to do with interpersonal relationships and the lack of support they received.

HOW FAITH CHANGES AMONG PARENTS WITH TRANSGENDER CHILDREN

As Christian parents navigate gender identity considerations with a child, their faith is often challenged in ways similar to those we have been describing among parents whose children identify as gay or lesbian. One additional challenge that typically arises for parents of transgender children is that less is written in Scripture about transgender experiences, gender dysphoria, or atypical experiences of gender identity. In our experience, most parents who believe Scripture proscribes same-sex behavior also extend those proscriptions to any kind of cross-gender or other gender identity or expression. Just as we see some parents questioning the sinfulness of same-sex attraction (and in some cases behavior) and others positively affirming that such behavior is not sinful, we similarly encounter parents who are questioning their beliefs about gender identity and expression as well as parents who believe transgender identity and cross-gender expression are not sinful. Some parents also find it helpful to distinguish a child's unchosen experience from their response to that experience; they may see gender incongruence as a reality that exists, perhaps as a result of the fall, but as not sinful. However, other parents may believe a child is doing wrong by just experiencing such incongruence.

A mother of a transgender son (a biological female who identifies as a boy) shared: "The only thing that changed is that I refuse to accept the fact that [transgender identity] is evil or a sin. I refuse to accept that. If people say, 'Well God made [your] little girl,' I tell people, very vocally, 'Yeah, and that little girl never felt right.'"[a]

Another layer of complexity in these parents' spiritual journey is how little the people around them typically know about transgender experiences and gender dysphoria. The experience of gender dysphoria is often confused with homosexuality in ways that are unhelpful to parents. Fewer resources are written about gender identity considerations from a Christian perspective, making it that much more challenging for parents to know how to proceed, especially when they face time-sensitive decisions at different stages of their child's development, such as whether to utilize puberty blockers at the early stages of pubertal development. These can be exceptionally difficult decisions for parents in general and for Christian parents in particular. These questions are not just medical or psychiatric but also spiritual for many parents; they need support as they pray for discernment and seek to parent in ways that are pleasing to God.

Positive and negative religious coping. Before we leave this section on Christian parents' spiritual journeys, we want to note how spiritual journeys are often tied to religious coping activities. Coping activities may be positive—such as talking to a friend or exercising—or they may be negative—such as turning to alcohol or becoming violent. Religious coping activities are coping activities that reflect a person's reliance on religious or spiritual resources or experiences of the transcendent. Like other coping activities, religious coping activities can be either positive or negative.

> *Like other coping activities, religious coping activities can be either positive or negative.*

We have already discussed several positive religious coping activities above: turning to God through prayer, reading Scripture, participating in religious community, and otherwise seeking direction or guidance from God. Negative religious coping activities might include feeling resentment toward God or feeling abandoned by God. Unsurprisingly, positive religious coping activities are generally associated with better mental health outcomes over time.[17] The same correlation between positive religious coping behaviors and better mental health outcomes seems to exist among Christian parents responding to a child's coming out. These positive coping behaviors can help parents work through early stages of grief and uncertainty, contributing to improvement over time for most parents. Conversely, as Erspamer notes, sustained negative religious coping can be tied to an increase in symptoms of depression and a decrease in life satisfaction in general.[18]

It is important for people in relationship with Christian parents to normalize the potentially tumultuous nature of these parents' journeys, including their spiritual journeys, especially early on after a child's disclosure of same-sex sexuality. A tumultuous journey is not an indictment on parents, their faith, or their child. Allow and encourage Christian parents to process negative emotions toward God, to work through feelings such as grief, and to ask hard spiritual questions. Be available to them, as they need time and space and support along the way.

LYNN AND GREG McDONALD ON HOW THEIR FAITH CHANGED OVER TIME

I (Lynn) continued to go to God daily asking him to show me what he wanted me to see. Were my beliefs and values right in God's eyes? Was there something I was missing or misunderstood pertaining to my beliefs about homosexuality? I once believed that if a person was living a homosexual life and did not repent, he/she should be shunned, not allowed to be a member of the church. Today I believe differently because of working through the questions above. Jesus never shunned any sinner. His words were always meant for restoration. Never to hurt or harm, but to bring hope and freedom from sin. In time we realized sanctification does not happen overnight, not in my life or my son's life. The Holy Spirit convicts us of our sins and things he wants to change in our life in his time, not mine.

As Jesus followers, we are called to be imitators of Jesus. Lynn and I (Greg) decided to go back and spend some time in the Gospels and asked ourselves four questions as we began studying the life of Jesus. Who did he say he was? Who did Jesus hang out with? How did he treat people? What did he have to say? This little exercise revealed so much to us about Jesus and how to love as he did. If Jesus was due north, we were due south in how we had been responding to Greg Jr. We became very serious about emulating Jesus.

Another aha moment was studying Matthew 22:36-40, when Matthew records this event where one of the Pharisees, an expert in the law, tested Jesus and asked this question: "Teacher, which is the greatest commandment in the Law?" Jesus replied: "'Love the Lord your God with all your heart and with all your soul and with all your mind.' This is the first and greatest commandment. And the second is like it: 'Love your neighbor as yourself.' All the Law and the Prophets hang on these two commandments." If Jesus was commanding us to love God and our neighbor, how much more our son! Today, when we are not sure what to do, we fall back on love. At the end of the day, it is not about being right; it is about being right with God.

> *"Today, when we are not sure what to do, we fall back on love."*

PARENTS' BELIEFS ABOUT HOMOSEXUALITY

Parents' beliefs about homosexuality often play an important role in the broader spiritual journey of Christian parents after a child comes out. For instance, Darnell and Deja, whom we introduced you to at the beginning of this chapter, never really questioned their belief that same-sex sexual behavior is sinful; however, they came to view same-sex attractions as just a part of their daughter's experience, something she never chose and would now have to figure out in light of her faith. Rather than struggling with their view of sexual ethics, Darnell and Deja struggled with how to receive support from their local faith community, particularly their pastor, and with broader questions about God's sovereignty. Let's turn our attention, then, to the ways Christian parents have expressed their beliefs about homosexuality and whether those beliefs have changed over time.

We've divided parents' views into three major categories: (1) the belief that same-sex sexual behavior (and possibly same-sex orientation as well) is a sin, (2) questioning of the belief that same-sex sexual behavior is a sin, and (3) the belief that same-sex sexual behavior is not a sin.

THE BELIEF THAT SAME-SEX SEXUAL BEHAVIOR IS A SIN

The belief that same-sex sexual behavior (and possibly same-sex orientation as well) is a sin was the belief most commonly held by Christian parents we interviewed prior to them learning that their child was gay. This is the view of most Christian parents who are part of a conservative Christian denomination. In the months following disclosure, the belief most frequently cited by the Christian parents we interviewed was questioning of their belief that same-sex sexual behavior was a sin. Other parents remained confident in this view, while still others remained confident in their view that same-sex sexual behavior was not a sin.

At the time we interviewed parents, an average of four years after their child came out to them as gay, we saw a spectrum of beliefs similar to the spectrum a few months after disclosure. The Christian parents we interviewed were most likely to be questioning the belief that same-sex sexual behavior was a sin. The second most common position among parents was the belief that this behavior was a sin. Parents were least likely to hold the belief that same-sex sexual behavior was not a sin.

In our most recent survey, 86% of Christian parents held a traditional view of same-sex sexual behavior as sinful prior to their child's disclosure of same-sex sexuality.[19] At the time they completed our survey (an average of five years after their child's disclosure), 35% of this group reported that their beliefs had shifted from a traditional view to an affirming view, while the majority (65%) reported that their beliefs had not shifted away from a traditional view.

Some parents also found it helpful to distinguish between sexual behavior and same-sex orientation or attraction. In our most recent survey, a sizable minority (about 40%) of Christian parents believed that same-sex attraction itself was sin prior to their child's coming out. Since their child came out, 59% of the group that held that belief reported a change in their view that same-sex attraction itself was sin. While most still held traditional beliefs about sexual behavior, they had a more nuanced understanding of the reality of same-sex attraction, coming to see it as an experience their child had not chosen and was not sinning by experiencing.

It is difficult to say how representative these samples are of Christian parents more broadly. However, we have seen that parents do sometimes experiences changes in belief over time, or at least begin to question beliefs once held confidently, after a child's coming out. We have also seen that some parents find it valuable after a child's coming out to carefully distinguish sexual behavior from sexual attraction or orientation.

Unsurprisingly, Christian parents who held the belief that homosexuality (whether sexual behavior or sexual orientation) was a sin tended to seek out resources from others who supported that same position. These parents were unlikely to seek out resources from individuals or organizations whose beliefs about sexuality and sexual behavior they considered too permissive or liberal. A subset of these parents also held the belief that, while same-sex sexual behavior was a sin, it was not worse than any other sin. A mother shared this theme in one of our interviews: "I know God loves the human being as a person but He doesn't accept the sin. This is just like any other sin. Whether you are homosexual or not, a sin is a sin, so how am I supposed to view this as God would view it?"[20]

Another mother of a gay child described how her shift in belief had led her to a similar view: "I still feel like that intimate physical relationship between people of the same sex is not God's ideal. The way I've changed is that to me, it's just a sin like any other sin. If we're going to let a glutton be a leader or teach in the church, then how do we decide which sins you're committing make it to where you can't be involved in the church? I struggle with that."[21]

While some parents remained confident in their view that same-sex sexual behavior was sinful, others began to question this belief.

Questioning the sinfulness of same-sex sexual behavior was the most common response of Christian parents whose child came out to them as gay.

QUESTIONING THE BELIEF THAT SAME-SEX SEXUAL BEHAVIOR IS A SIN

Throughout our interviews, we saw many parents question the belief that same-sex sexual behavior is a sin. But our use of the word *questioning* may not always capture the depth of the anguish parents experienced as so many of their previously held beliefs were shaken. Here is a mother who expressed well how her son's coming out shook her faith:

> It rocked my faith to its very core. Nothing had ever shaken my faith so much. I was angry at first. I just didn't know how to handle it. It totally shook my faith. I didn't lose my faith. I knew what I believed in. I knew I was Christian, but everything was different when it came to my faith. I started seeing what my son had seen from the beginning because I was keeping this secret and going to church and hearing things. It really rocked my faith to the core.[22]

Here is an example of a father who reflected on how his views have shifted, making room for previously unasked questions:

> I have some questions now that I didn't have before. Five years ago, I would have told you that I was certain: Homosexuality is a sin, they're going to hell, and that's the end of it. I can't say that they're not going to hell now, but I can't say that they're not going to heaven either. Right now, I'm teetering on the fence. I would have told you five years ago that there is no way an LGBT person could be a Christian and live that lifestyle. I now think you can be a follower of Christ and a homosexual at the same time. Just like you can be a Christian and stuck in gossip, lying, pornography. I'm much more open right now to the Holy Spirit filling and leading me with the whole lifestyle.[23]

Among Christian parents who were questioning the belief that homosexuality (whether sexual behavior or sexual orientation) was a sin, there was a tendency to seek multiple perspectives on the topic of homosexuality. We noted above that when parents believe that homosexuality is a sin, they tend to look to resources that share their perspective. But parents who question that belief tend to cast a broader net when it comes to looking for biblical studies and other resources on the topic of sexual identity. Here a parent reflects on the questions raised by her child's coming out; she also shares how she began to look into multiple perspectives on biblical interpretation:

> The longer you deal with [the topic of homosexuality], the more you hear other people's interpretations of the Bible and what is most consistent with Jesus' message; it adds a lot of grey. Whereas before it was more black-and-white, now it's more grey. I think I'm more willing to accept that grey stuff than [my husband] is. I'm open to seeing that there is some space in there. I do appreciate that there have been some ways that even our modern translations [of the Bible] have been skewed toward our black-and-white view as opposed to using more open language. Those things are all evolving. I'm not anywhere right now. I'm a really mushy person when it comes to talking about this. I'm like, "God knows and only God knows." To be honest, that's how I feel right now. My main thing is, "If you have those [same-sex attraction] issues in your heart, just be in touch with God because God is going to tell you what is right for you. It might not be the same as what is right for somebody else. You just have to stay close to God." That is the only thing I can say with confidence.[24]

While most parents we interviewed were either convinced of a traditional sexual ethic or questioning that belief, we also interviewed a smaller number of parents who held the belief that same-sex sexual behavior was not a sin. Let's take a look at their experience.

THE BELIEF THAT SAME-SEX
SEXUAL BEHAVIOR IS NOT A SIN

Christian parents who reached the conclusion that same-sex sexual behavior was not a sin tended to consider changing churches to be in a place of worship that reflected gay-affirming theology. Here is one mother who describes how her views changed regarding homosexuality, and how her change in views led her and her husband to change churches:

> We wound up joining the Episcopal Church rather than going back to the evangelical church. Our denomination has changed. My relationship with God has pretty much always been the same, since I became a Christian. . . . I've come to feel that there are a lot of people who are good Christians no matter what denomination they are in. Specifically, as to people being gay, I don't think that it's sinful anymore. I don't think God thinks it's sinful anymore.[25]

Christian parents who held the belief that same-sex sexual behavior was not a sin also typically held the view that God made their child this way. Here is an example of a father who described the shift in his views about same-sex sexual behavior by referencing the conviction that homosexuality is who a person is: "So yeah, my views have changed. On this particular issue, they've changed from 'Homosexuality is an abomination and sinful,' to where they are now, which is that God's not judging people on that. That's who you are. What a shame that you might feel that God doesn't love you because of who you are."[26]

Beliefs about homosexuality are an important part of Christian parents' experience throughout their journey with a child who comes out as gay. Although most of the Christian parents we interviewed held to a traditional view regarding same-sex sexual behavior, some parents reported a shift in their beliefs after their child came out to them. But beliefs, as important as they are, represent only part of a larger spiritual journey that we wanted to consider in this chapter.

> *Beliefs, as important as they are,*
> *represent only part of a larger spiritual journey.*

We mentioned above that being part of a local faith community is a significant aspect of many Christian parents' spiritual journey. We want to revisit the experience of parents in church, as this topic is complex for many parents and can be a source of great anguish.

CHURCH REVISITED

In one of our projects, we examined Christian parents in relation to their local church community.[27] In a study of over two hundred Christian parents, about 60% of parents indicated that they stayed in the church they had been a part of before their child came out. The remaining parents (approximately 40%) who left their church typically did so because they liked aspects of their new church or because their previous church proved difficult for them to stay a part of after their child came out. Most of these parents who left a church community did so after sharing with that community about their child being gay. They reported to us a range of responses they received from that community before their departure, responses that in some cases help explain their decision to seek another church.

As we noted, the majority of parents we interviewed stayed in the church they were a part of when their child came out to them as gay. Their reasons for staying varied considerably. Some parents were already fairly involved in their church, and that investment was not something they were going to just set aside. For other parents whose views were gay affirming (or whose views shifted to a gay-affirming position), they stayed in their church to effect change in that church's stance toward LGBTQ+ persons. Even among parents who held traditional views about sexual ethics, many chose to stay in their church in order to help their church have compassion toward young people navigating same-sex sexuality and faith. Still other parents wanted to be a resource to fellow parents in their church.

For example, one parent shared with us, "We decided to stay for the time being because we can have influence if the topic comes up."[28] Similarly, another parent shared their decision-making process in choosing to remain in a nonaffirming church despite their own affirming beliefs: "There are times where I have considered being part of more progressive congregation, but I have taken efforts to move our congregation to be more open and affirming. They are moving in that direction."[29]

Other parents have reflected on what they did not receive from their church and wondered whether they could be a resource to other parents facing similar circumstances. For instance, here is one father's response when asked whether his family had changed churches since his child's coming out:

No. [My wife] and I have talked about that from time to time. We are waiting on two things. I want to sit down and have my pastor talk with me. We used to talk frequently and he was very close with [my son]. Since [my son] came out, I haven't had a conversation with him one way or the other, whatsoever. I have been waiting for him to pull me aside, but he hasn't. Part of me thinks I should sit down and share with him about how I see myself as someone who can be a resource in the church and in the community for people who are going through the same thing. I see it as an opportunity.[30]

Many parents do not experience support from their local church. This father noted that his pastor had not spoken to him since his son had come out. Recall that Darnell and Deja, from our opening story, struggled with whether they could approach their pastor because of how he had previously discussed the topic of same-sex sexuality. Experiences like these are not uncommon for parents.

Several parents we interviewed were in the midst of decision-making about whether to stay in their current church or find a new faith community. One mother shared how her child's coming out affected her family's roles in their church:

Years ago, when we became members, part of the membership vow was saying that homosexuality was wrong, and we said, "Yeah whatever." Now we know that we can't be in the kind of leadership that we have been [in the past]. If this issue comes up, we will have to determine whether we will stay silent, or speak to it, or let [our son's] story out. [My husband] is no longer able to be a deacon or elder. We can't be in major leadership any longer because of [our son]. That's cool with us, but it is kind of sad too. We're working through whether or not we should stay there. It has been our church home for almost ten years and been so important to us. Our

[Christian] friendships and our whole church life are in that setting, but it may not be possible to be there [anymore]. [Our son] said, "Don't do that because of me. You still do good work there. Don't let one issue be the deal." So that's something we are wrestling with, particularly in our friendships with our closest friends, who know about [our son] and love him and us but can't embrace his homosexuality. That's the tricky part right now for us.[31]

This mother's account of her family's church experience raises a number of important issues. She captures the heartache of considering leaving a church after ten years; the integrity necessary to step down from leadership roles due to conflicts in belief, while being willing to stay engaged in order to voice disagreement or dissent; the potential guilt her son may experience should they leave their church because of his same-sex sexuality; whether to continue serving in a setting where important points of disagreement remain; and so much more. There are no easy answers to these complex issues. If you are facing similarly complex questions, please know that it is not uncommon to grapple with a range of considerations related to your local faith community.

> *There are no easy answers to these complex issues.*

You will recall that while most parents reported that they remained in their church as of the time we interviewed them (about four years, on average, post-disclosure), about 40% of parents changed churches after their child came out. Parents left for a variety of reasons, but often they shared that they felt isolated, uncomfortable, or judged.

A mother of a daughter who came out as gay shared, "The church wasn't helping us. I turned away—not from God—from going to church. I did not feel comfortable telling people that I have a gay daughter because I was afraid. . . . In my case, I stopped going to church and I didn't want to be around people. I fell into a depression. I was mostly a loner."[32]

Some parents described painful encounters—experiences of hearing hurtful words or feeling degraded by others. For example, one mother shared, "We don't go to church where we used to. I let my husband lead the way, but we are somewhere where I don't think you'll hear the belligerent speech and degradation of anybody that doesn't agree with them."[33]

Hurtful words were often especially hurtful when they were directed toward the same-sex-oriented child. A mother shared, "I don't want to go to a church where they see my son as a mistake and they don't see him as a child of God. That is unacceptable to me."[34]

Other parents shared similar experiences of hearing teaching on the topic of homosexuality differently in light of their child having come out to them: "I've never been ashamed of anything [my daughter's] done, but it was really hard to go to church and have the preacher preach on homosexuality. It was really hard to sit and listen to him condemn my child for something he knew nothing about. I guess it was just harder [after my daughter came out]."[35]

Sometimes, after one parent experiences great hurt, a couple decides together to leave the church they have been a part of. For example, a mother of a gay child shared her decision to leave with her husband, who was being hurt in their church: "He'd also been on the elder board at the church we'd been to for a long time and felt beat up and needed something else. . . . It washed over his soul and I went along for the ride. I hadn't been hurt in ministry like he had been. I reluctantly went along to [the new church] on Saturday nights."[36]

In addition to married couples leaving churches in order to be able to attend the same church together, families also sometimes sought out a new church because of their desire to go to church as a whole family or to ensure that their adult child could attend the same church with the parents when they were home. One father expressed the desire to be able to attend church together with his gay son: "I don't want to go to a church and have them condemn homosexuality because I want [my son] to go with me."[37]

Even more conservative Christian parents struggled with whether to stay in their church because they did not feel there was adequate support for them. The journey they were on was often not a journey others were willing to support them in. One parent spoke of their desire and efforts to stay at their church amid the inadequacy of the church's response: "We tried to stay, but it got lonelier and lonelier there because people didn't know how to deal with our grief. They started avoiding us."[38]

Although most of those who left their church found another church to join instead, some left organized church itself, while others left Christianity altogether. Neither of these results were commonly reported, but they did occur for some families. When families left a church and did not elect to go to another church (but found other ways to be in Christian fellowship and in ministry), this decision seemed to reflect their frustration with "organized" church.[39] One father shared what this decision looked like for his family:

> It's been a little over three years [since my son came out]. We spent about a year and a half struggling with our church to see if we could influence them to understand some things a little better. With that having failed, we walked away from the organized church completely. . . . We still are members of small groups and are involved in Christian outreach. We still have a strong faith, pray, and read the Bible.[40]

Still other parents, though not many of those we interviewed, reported that they had left their faith altogether. One parent shared, "I don't go to church anymore. I don't believe the myths. I do believe in God, but not in the God that I learned to believe in when I was going to church or growing up. It's more of a great spirit, or maybe it's nature. I'm not sure. I don't really have a name for it, but I do not believe in myths of the divinity of Jesus of Nazareth. I do not believe in any of that stuff anymore."[41]

Positive experience in church. If parents did leave their old church and join a different church, what did they say they gained in their new church? In our research, we have been most struck by the sense of acceptance parents said they gained in their new church. According to Sides, parents' experience of acceptance is not necessarily related to affirmation of same-sex relationships but is an experience of a church being "welcoming, loving, and friendly towards" gay persons.[42] Churches where these parents thrived showed respect to others who were different.

Here is an example of a mother describing her experience with a new church: "The Holy Spirit was telling me [my son] was made this way and that I needed to get away from a church that doesn't believe that. We found the new church, and it's a more loving atmosphere. It is Lutheran. [My son] loves going to church and says the people are friendly to him and the pastor is always engaging to him. Of course, the pastor does know about [my son]."[43]

This mother's response points specifically to the question of what a church believes about why same-sex sexuality occurs. More broadly, her favorable view of her new church has to do with its friendly and loving climate.

A mother of a gay son shared how important her women's Bible study and other relational connections were in providing her with tangible support:

> My women's Bible study, as a support group, was the best thing I found through this whole thing. Other people who have [a gay child] or that can help you through it are the best resources for me. Friends and other people that I have met in the process, that have been able to sit and say, "I know what you are going through and this is my experience," [have been great]. . . . I was just looking for someone to come up to me and say, "I don't have much to say, but I'm going to give you a hug." Knowing that somebody else went this way before and getting a prayer and a hug was the best thing for me. That's what helped me through so much of it.[44]

Another parent, a father, shared his experience and the experience of his family as they changed churches:

> The new church is a larger church . . . a very dynamic, growing church. It's still conservative, but we work hard to make anybody feel welcome who comes into the entry level, that is, into the worship experience. We don't make a lot of issues a gate. We have a lot of people that have a lot of brokenness in their lives, and we don't make that something that they have to overcome before they

can get involved. . . . . I feel like my core belief and interpretation of scripture concerning sexuality is the same, but certainly my practice is much more full of grace.[45]

Among the parents we surveyed who moved to a new church, many sought out a more loving church environment while retaining a traditional Christian sexual ethic. However, other parents shared about their move to a more progressive or gay-affirming church. For instance, one parent shared, "I started searching for gay-affirming churches and found one in the area. I met with the pastor. I said, 'I know you are a gay-affirming church, but what do you believe as far as gay and lesbian people?' It's a female pastor. She said she believes that God made them that way. I cried, because my faith is very important to me and I want [my son] to keep his faith."[46]

Another parent shared about finding love and acceptance in a gay-affirming church: "I decided that what [my daughter] needed was a nice dose of loving, accepting Christianity. I moved us to an Episcopal church in town that's very open and gay friendly. In order to protect her heart and in order to have a constant influence of loving, accepting gay friend Christians in her life, I decided to [change churches]. She doesn't need to fight church."[47]

Whether to "come out" at church. If you are a parent reading this book, you may be asking yourself whether you want to share your story at your church. You aren't alone. Although three-fourths of the parents we interviewed did share their story with someone at their church, about one-quarter of those we interviewed had not done so.

For many parents, the decision not to disclose their child's sexuality had to do with the perspective that this story was their child's own story, something their child could choose to share when they felt ready. One parent explained:

I chose not to [tell people my son is gay]. I just think it is not everyone's business. I think it should not be that big of a deal. It is just part of who you are, and you shouldn't have to wear it on your sleeve. [My son] didn't try to keep it a secret from people at school, but he didn't tell people in the church community. I said to myself, "It is [my son's] job to come out or not come out, not mine."[48]

For those parents who did decide to disclose their child's coming out to someone in their church, this decision was typically measured and thoughtful. These parents tended to share with those they handpicked and trusted. This group of trusted people may have included pastors or church leaders, people in a cell group or Bible study, or other close friends. Although most of our parents reported positive responses after disclosure, many also reported negative responses; parents often had a mixture of experiences.

It was not uncommon for church-based confidants, whether pastors or other leaders or friends, to offer to pray for the parents and their child. One parent remembers: "We cried together and they said that they would pray for us and him. With the youth pastor it was the same thing. He was very sad and said that he'd pray for us."[49] Others said people just listened to them and were quietly present with them: "Some people were just so sweet and quiet. They didn't have much to say and just were there."[50]

Negative responses often took the form of "pat answers" and oversimplifications, such as suggesting that a gay son just needed to meet the "right girl."[51] Other negative experiences occurred when a parent's vulnerable sharing was met with silence or isolation. Some parents found themselves being ignored by people they had been in fellowship with the week prior.

One mother detailed an especially painful unfolding of events at her church:

> You start slowly telling people and then you find out that they knew all along. Then you find out that is how they define you. They say, "Here are [the interviewee] and [her husband]. They're the ones with the gay son." It's like a wart on our nose. I've had people come up to me and say [condescendingly], "How's [your son]? How are you?" I would overhear things like, "Those homosexuals ruined everything." It's all around you. I can't stand it. I know who

approves of us and who doesn't. Some that say they approve; I don't really know [whether they do]. It's hard.[52]

A mother discussed what it was like for her to share about her child's sexuality with her pastor and not hear from him again, leading to feelings of hurt and anger:

The hard part is that some of the people we told (like our pastor) haven't really gotten back to us and asked us how we're doing in this area. It bugs the crap out of us. We shared it with our pastor early on, and he hasn't revisited it at all. People don't know what to say and do with this topic. The fact that our pastor hasn't followed up with us has made a difference, especially with my husband. He's hurt. Because the pastor is a friend, [my husband] felt we needed to tell them; in hindsight, I wouldn't have. I think there's some anger in us towards our church. Anger sometimes comes from hurt, and I think the bottom emotion is hurt.[53]

Another mother shared a similar, painful experience with a pastor. Her pain, however, was motivated not by her pastor's silence but by his hurtful words:

I could not deal with it. I told my husband I couldn't continue to go there and that it felt like it's against my soul. It just so happened that [our son] had gone to church with us a couple times there. Thankfully every time [our pastor] had mentioned the homosexual piece and had talked against it, my son was not sitting beside me. I thank God for that. This time it was more than I could stomach. I actually sent [the pastor] an email because he offended me and it felt hateful. . . . It felt like there was so much hate in what he was saying, and it felt like the entire body was being taught to hate homosexuals. I attend Bible study still at my old church. I finally told my Bible group about the letter [I had written to the pastor]. A couple of them actually attend that church and they told me I needed to send it. I prayed over it. I sent it to my group leader. I told her I didn't want to appear psycho. She said it was beautiful and it was obviously from my heart and she encouraged me to send it. I prayed about it and got the go-ahead and I sent the email to the pastor. He replied back, and it was all downhill from there. He related homosexuality to child molesters and alcoholics and drug abusers. It was like I was going through the whole thing all over again. I cried for days. I have not been back to church since. I feel like I'm still looking for a home.[54]

Despite these negative stories, we also heard about many positive experiences parents had in their churches. These positive experiences most often came not in an organized, top-down way but from the grassroots, through the organic support of friends whom parents felt they could trust with their story.

Some parents reported receiving support and encouragement from people in their home group or Bible study and from other friends. Sometimes this support was as simple as expressing a desire for the gay child to remain at their church. One parent reported: "Everybody that I have told, urged [my son] to come back [to church]. They were sad that he felt like he couldn't come. They were sad that he felt like he would be judged. They wanted him to come back. Of course, I can't say what they would say or where they would try to steer him if he did come back."[55]

Regardless of the specific contents of the positive responses parents received from their faith community, these responses were all loving, supportive, and nonjudgmental. And these individual responses tended to influence how parents perceived their welcome in the faith community as a whole. Experiences at church—for good or for ill—are interpersonally mediated.

> *Experiences at church—for good or for ill— are interpersonally mediated.*

One parent explained how freeing it was to feel the support of her church: "I just felt like I had church family that I could talk to. I could share things about [my daughter's] life in our Bible studies and not feel judged at all. I felt like my Bible study partners were very supportive. It was good to have someone to talk to. I don't have any secrets. I have to be with people that are willing to deal with that."[56]

Another mother shared about her positive experience at her home church:

> The majority of them that have said anything to me have been very sympathetic and nonjudgmental. I think it's because we've been in this fellowship of believers for twenty-five years. Most of these women that are commenting to me at all changed [my son's] diapers. They love him. Every time [my son] comes to town, he is sitting right next to me on the pews, singing praise and worship. I said, "You can never say you felt judgment at our church," because these people love him.[57]

JEAN COLES ON HOW HER FAITH CHANGED OVER TIME

I've grown in understanding that homosexuality is often, and sadly, a lonely road for people in the church. It's understandable that many who are oriented this way wouldn't be attracted to Christianity. Even if someone is choosing to follow Jesus in all things, and concluding that sex between those of the same gender is prohibited, they still often face a lot of rejection. This is tragic!

I've also grown in understanding that switching one's orientation may not be possible. This means that we need to accept people who are gay and learn from them. The church has overpromoted marriage as a goal and downplayed singleness and celibacy. No one should feel like a second-class Christian. God lives in all followers of Jesus.

ADVICE FROM CHRISTIAN PARENTS

Reflect on what you believe. We saw at the opening of this chapter that beliefs about homosexuality are an important starting point for many Christian parents. Regardless of what you currently believe, it can be helpful, as many parents have suggested, to reflect on what you believe and to know why you believe what you believe.

We noted, too, that some parents found it helpful to distinguish between sexual behavior and same-sex attraction or orientation. Indeed, most Christian parents did not view the experience of same-sex attraction as a sin their child was committing but just as a part of their experience, something they did not choose. We see this approach as representing a more nuanced understanding of sexuality, sexual behavior, and sexual attraction or orientation. In our experience, we have not seen people choose to experience attraction to the same sex; rather, a small percentage of people find themselves attracted to the same sex as they go through puberty, just as people who are heterosexual find themselves attracted to the opposite sex. Distinguishing attraction or orientation from behavior is often helpful.

You may be questioning traditional beliefs about same-sex sexual behavior and relationships. It is certainly permissible to ask questions of God in this moment and all along your journey. God is able to hear our questions and sit with us in silence as we wonder how to make sense of all that is going on at present.

It is also a good idea to know why you believe what you believe, and perhaps to consider why others believe as they do. One parent shared with us in our recent survey, "Although my views haven't changed, I have learned more about the arguments on the progressive side and know they are trying to act with compassion."[58]

When Christians have not given their own beliefs much thought, their beliefs can sometimes come across to others as mere prejudice. If your beliefs and convictions about sexuality do not reflect thoughtful deliberation, it could be helpful for you to reflect on why you believe what you believe, so that there is a substantive dimension to your convictions. It is also perfectly understandable to be uncertain of what you believe—to have questions that have arisen for you in this journey and to live with some of those questions or points of tension.

Take the long view. One of the most important pieces of advice parents have offered has to do with having realistic expectations about your entire journey with your child. One parent advised, "Don't panic. Realize, as a lot of resources told me and I didn't want to hear, that this is going to be a long process. At that point, I believed the process they were referring to was the process of [my son] being healed. Now, I believe it's a process of me being healed. That's a long process. Do not latch on to anything as 'the fix.' It's going to take some time."[59]

While we do not know all the details of what "healing" this mother was referring to, this is clearly a woman who can attest to the idea of a journey unfolding over time, crossing unexpected terrain that is both unexpected and unexpectedly beautiful.

Find pockets of safety and support. We noted above that most of the parents we interviewed and surveyed were more conservative, holding to a traditional Christian sexual ethic. For many parents, the coming-out experience led them to question these beliefs. Most parents end up staying in their local church community, and they wanted that community to become a safer place for them, for their child, and for others navigating similar circumstances.

Toward that end, it may be helpful for you to identify a few people with whom you can be honest about what has been happening, about your own beliefs and questions, about your church's teaching on the topic of sexuality and sexual behavior, and so on. In other words, find pockets of safety and vulnerability so that others you trust can join you on the journey. These friends represent pockets of safety by providing you with emotionally and spiritually safe relationships where you can sort out your thoughts, questions, and emotions without being told what to believe or how to feel. Your journey can be healthier when you are properly supported and able to work out your own convictions in an intellectually honest and emotionally safe way.

YOUR TURN: HOW FAITH CHANGES OVER TIME

Take some time at the end of this chapter to reflect on a few questions related to how faith changes over time:

- Many Christian parents we interviewed held the belief that homosexuality (either sexual behavior or sexual orientation) was a sin. Other parents questioned that belief over time. Still others did not view homosexuality (either sexual behavior or sexual orientation) as a sin. What do you believe? Do you distinguish attractions or orientation from behavior? Why or why not?

- Many Christian parents described their spiritual journey with respect to experiences in prayer, Scripture reading, trust in God, and participation in a local faith community. How you seen shifts in your spiritual journey over time in these or other areas?

- How has your local faith community been a resource to you? If it has not been as much of a resource as you had hoped, how would you like to respond to that deficit? How and where will you meet some of your needs for local Christian fellowship and support?

6

HOW PARENTS COME
TO TERMS WITH REALITY

Ryan and Raegan are in their midforties. They came to us for a consultation because their oldest daughter, Remi, age eighteen, had come out as gay about a year prior. In the early stages of counseling, we focused on how they learned that Remi was gay, which happened when they came across comments on some pictures posted on social media. They asked Remi about the comments and she shared that she was, in fact, gay; she hadn't said anything to them because she didn't know how to talk about it. Remi said she was worried they would be upset with her because of how LGBTQ+ people are sometimes talked about at their church and even in their home on occasion. We discussed Ryan and Raegan's regrets about how they had first reacted to Remi's coming out. They had confronted her about the comments on social media with a critical tone, and then, after learning she was gay, challenged whether Remi was telling the truth because she had dated a boy the previous year and had planned to go to prom with another boy. Remi felt defensive and responded with either sarcasm or silence and withdrawal. Communication fell off precipitously. Remi was willing to join us for counseling a few times to help with communication and to share more about her experiences. She described her first awareness of same-sex attraction and how she made sense of her sexuality. She explained her reasons for planning to go to prom with a guy: she wasn't attracted to this guy (or to any guy), but she'd been trying to avoid the awkward conversations they were now having as a family. She also shared that she had dated a boy two years ago to see whether she could be attracted to the opposite sex. Although communication

improved between Ryan, Raegan, and Remi, challenges still persisted re-
lated to Ryan and Raegan's hope that Remi's sexuality was a "phase"
rather than an enduring reality. It wasn't until several months later that
Raegan acknowledged in counseling that Remi was really gay: "I need to
really get that [she is gay] and let that sink in so I can think and plan and
prepare for the future. I've got to stop mentally going to that place where
all of this goes away. Where all of it was just a dream."

What we call "coming to terms with reality" is an experience that occurs as parents' relationship with their child changes over time—as initial challenges subside and the parent-child relationship resumes its pre-disclosure quality, or rises to a better quality, in terms of dynamics such as communication and authenticity. These and other intangibles culminate in parents' awareness that they have reached a stasis point, what some parents refer to as the new normal.[1]

In this stage, parents are no longer holding on to the fantasy that same-sex sexuality is just a phase their child is going through. They're no longer clinging to the fact that their child went to prom with someone of the opposite sex as proof that their child really is straight and will eventually revert to straightness. Similarly, for parents of transgender kids, there is a coming to terms with the reality of their child's experience of their gender.

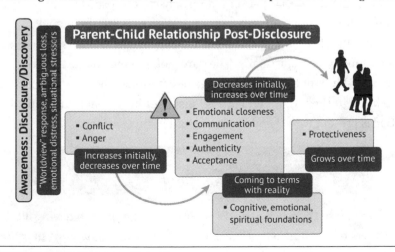

Figure 6.1. Coming to terms with reality

In one study of Christian parents, we described parents' experience this way:

> In the later phase parents began to integrate and accept a new relationship with their child. . . . Parents worked toward coming to terms with a new reality and integrating this into their understanding of their world, beliefs, values, and future. We see this as an attempt to restore congruence and homeostasis. . . . Much like the process of separation and individuation, this is a time in which the parent and child strengthened healthy boundaries and grew in respect for one another.[2]

Parents who experience what we refer to as coming to terms with reality do not necessarily report that they have everything figured out or that there are no conflicts or value differences between them and their child. That's not what we mean by coming to terms with reality. Instead, parents who enter this phase are in a better place to figure out things eventually, allowing events to unfold and taking one day at a time. They are in a better place to identify the source of the conflicts they experience and to exercise prudence in deciding which concerns are most important to them and when to discuss those concerns. While they recognize potential value differences between themselves and their child, they can also see that fear-based responses to those value differences will probably not facilitate a better relationship with their child.

Parents who come to terms with reality are in a more settled place emotionally and spiritually. They are not as emotionally reactive, although they still experience a range of emotions. They are not as likely to be anguished by spiritual questions; they have peace and hope that God is present with them and their child in this journey.

> *Parents who come to terms with reality are in a more settled place emotionally and spiritually.*

Coming to terms with reality is not synonymous with having all the answers or reaching a destination in which every challenging question has been answered. Rather, it is a place of stability from which parents can explore their present and future questions in anticipation that God will provide answers and direction and will sustain them along the way. Let's consider how three main foundations of parenting—cognitive, emotional, and spiritual—interact with parents' experiences of coming to terms with their sexuality.

Cognitive foundations. The cognitive adjustment (or changes in how you think and related mental processes) that takes place for parents over time has to do with meaning making.[3] How a person makes meaning out of difficult circumstances is important. What attributions will a parent make about same-sex sexuality, their child, and their related circumstances? Cognitively, coming to terms with reality means moving from a place of confusion to a place of insight. This cognitive adjustment is profound and is informed by a parent's Christian worldview, but that worldview may also shift over time, as happened with many parents in our research. Some of the shifts that take place can be measured by the self-talk parents engage in that leads either to discouragement or to hope.

For parents like Ryan and Raegan, helpful self-talk includes acknowledging, "Our daughter, Remi, is gay. When she uses the word *gay*, she is saying she is attracted to women. She is telling us she has a more enduring, stable experience of same-sex sexuality." Ryan and Raegan are accepting the reality of what Remi has told them.

Helpful self-talk will also frame positively the fact that Remi is sharing more of herself with her parents.[4] Remi is saying that she prefers not to hide this part of her experience from her parents. She does not want to "live a lie." Ryan and Raegan might reflect to themselves, "We may not know how to respond or where to go from here, but we can at least agree that we are grateful Remi is willing to share this part of her life with us. She doesn't want to continue to hide this aspect of her experience from us. There is an integrity that goes along with that."

Discouraging and unhelpful self-talk might be, "Where did we go wrong? What did we do that caused Remi to be gay? We should have been clearer about what we thought of same-sex sexuality. We should have been more up front about our own convictions so she knew to take this option off the table." This kind of self-talk reduces Remi's same-sex sexuality to "willful disobedience," which does not account for how Remi came to find herself attracted to other girls when she went through puberty. It directs the parents' attention to searching for causal reasons that are largely unknown.

Ryan and Raegan might also find it helpful to counter some of their previous wishful thinking:

> If I'm honest with myself, I had hoped this was a teenager thing, a passing trend—nothing sustained, nothing real. But it is real. Remi is telling us it is real and that it has been a part of her experience for the past five years. It is an important part of her experience, and we are now in a position to know her better as she launches into emerging adulthood and as we shift to a more adult-to-adult relationship over time.

Parents' cognitive terrain shifts as they come to better understand experiences that were once confusing to them. For example,

> When Remi dated a boy a couple of years ago, it wasn't that she was straight and now she is gay; rather, she was dating to see if she was able to experience attraction to a boy, and because she believed that dating would make life easier both for her and for us. She also probably wanted to avoid some of the uncomfortable conversations we are now having about her same-sex sexuality. Her choice is beginning to make sense.

Another indicator of parents' coming to terms with reality is that they can recognize unhelpful, shame-producing self-talk based on erroneous theories and adaptively replace it with helpful self-talk. For example, Ryan and Raegan might have entertained shaming self-talk about the origins of Remi's sexuality: "I wonder if we should have kept Remi from playing for that one team. I knew the coach was gay and I had a sense it was not a good idea, but I just didn't take the time to pull her out of that league and get her plugged into another league." Instead, parents who have come to terms with reality begin to think in more healthy and adaptive ways: "I don't know what caused or contributed to my daughter experiencing same-sex attraction, but no one really knows how sexual orientation develops. I'm not alone in that."

Ryan and Raegan might also make cognitive adjustments when thinking about the challenges their daughter will face. They might say, "Remi will face many challenges in this next year—challenges we just did not have on our radar—but we want to be able to come alongside her and be a resource to her as she faces these challenges."

Similarly, Ryan and Raegan might make a cognitive adjustment regarding the decisions facing Remi. They might say, "Remi will face many decisions in the weeks and months ahead—decisions we have not faced ourselves and may not fully understand—but we want to be able to support her as she faces these decisions."

Cognitive adjustments such as these can function as a kind of foundation from which you can offer support to your child. By taking cognitive steps to come to terms with reality, you are positioning yourself next to your child as a resource and source of support and encouragement. This does not mean you will agree with every decision your child makes. Your own beliefs about what is morally permissible may remain the same, as they did for most of the parents we surveyed. You may have difficult conversations, value conflicts, and so on, as many parents have with their adult children from time to time. Even so, allowing room for cognitive adjustments tends to form an important role in parents' coming to terms with the reality of their child's same-sex sexuality.

DAVE COLES ON COMING TO TERMS WITH THE REALITY OF HIS SON'S SAME-SEX SEXUALITY

The cognitive change came through reading research showing that major changes in sexual orientation (from gay to straight) generally had not happened in the decisive way that those changes had been represented in the past. That fresh perspective cemented my thankfulness at how Greg had processed his journey and the conclusions he had reached. It also facilitated a shift from the measure of sadness I had felt (at the loss of my dreams for Greg) to an abundance of parental pride at his stand for radical discipleship in the context of who God has created him to be.

. . . I think that based on my best understanding ten years earlier, my fatherly and pastoral advice would have been less than helpful.

I suspect that with all sincere love and good intentions, I might well have offered suggestions and perspectives that would have been counterproductive. I might have not have handled the struggle with sufficient care, assuming it to be a phase that would pass. Or, faced with the ongoing reality of same-sex attraction, I would likely have encouraged earnest and expectant prayer for a change of orientation. Not that such prayer would have been inherently wrong, but it might have brought undue pressure and increased disappointment with God at unanswered prayer. So, while I felt sorry that Greg had walked the decade-plus journey alone, I praised God for his leading in Greg's processing and life choices.

Emotional foundations. The emotional adjustments parents make over time as they come to terms with reality fall into two broad categories. First, they make adjustments to reduce conflict and negative emotional experiences, by facing and working through grief and decreasing the frequency of fear-based parenting methods. Second, they grow in positive emotional experiences such as love, emotional closeness, and engagement, as well as in their experience of authenticity with their child.

Parents' reports of their emotional well-being over time can be an indicator of their coming to terms with reality. In our most recent survey, we asked Christian parents to complete the Depression, Anxiety, and Stress Scale (DASS-21). The DASS-21 looks at the severity of a person's experience of depression, anxiety, and stress, classifying results as in "the normal range," "mild," "moderate," "severe," or "extremely severe." As the publishers of the DASS-21 note, "The severity labels are used to describe the full range of scores in the population, so 'mild' for example means that the person is above the population mean but probably still way below the typical severity of someone seeking help (i.e., it does not mean a mild level of disorder)."[5] The DASS-21 is typically used to identify where a person might be at greatest risk among these three categories—that is, are they at greatest risk for depression, or in the area of anxiety, or in managing stress? The scores do not correspond to a diagnosis as such. However, greater severity scores in the area of depression are characteristically reported by people who are more "self-disparaging, dispirited, gloomy, blue, convinced that life has no meaning or value, pessimistic about the future, unable to experience enjoyment or satisfaction, unable to become interested or involved, slow, lacking in initiative."[6] Similarly, greater severity scores for anxiety would be characteristic of people who are "apprehensive, panicky, trembly, shaky, aware of dryness of the mouth, breathing difficulties, pounding of the heart, sweatiness of the palms, worried about performance and possible loss of control."[7] Finally, greater severity scores in the area of stress are characteristic of people who are "over-aroused, tense, unable to relax, touchy, easily upset, irritable, easily startled, nervy, jumpy, fidgety, intolerant of interruption or delay."[8]

We compared Christian parents who completed the DASS-21 and had a child come out within the past three years to Christian parents who had a child come out more than three years ago, looking for changes on the measure of depression, anxiety, and stress.[9]

Christian parents, early in their response to the coming-out experience, report a range of experiences of depression, including 21% reporting mild, 25% reporting moderate, and 17% reporting severe or extremely severe depression (see fig. 6.2). Note, however, that 37% of parents scored in the normal range. There is great variability among Christian parents within the first three years of the coming-out experience.

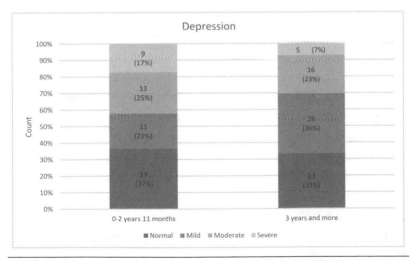

Figure 6.2. Comparison of parents with children who came out within three years (N=52) and parents with children who came out after three years or more (N=69) on measure of depression

Of the three areas measured by this scale, anxiety stands out to us (see fig. 6.3); 62% of Christian parents shortly after their child's coming out fell in the severe or extremely severe range for anxiety. When we compare these parents to Christian parents whose child came out to them three or more years previously, we see lower percentages of parents reporting severe anxiety; while 38% of parents still reported severe anxiety, this rate is much lower than the 62% rate among parents whose child came out more recently.

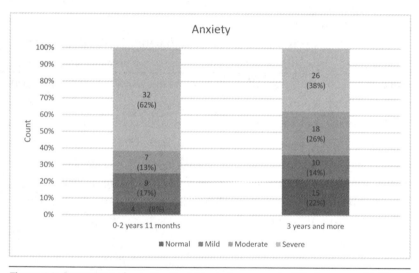

Figure 6.3. Comparison of parents with children who came out within three years (N=52) and parents with children who came out after three years or more (N=69) on measure of anxiety

The severity ratings for stress were interesting too, but for different reasons (see fig. 6.4). Compared to what we saw on measures of anxiety, in particular, relatively few parents reported mild, moderate, or severe stress either within the three years or three years and more following disclosure. We had 77% of parents in the normal range within the first three years following disclosure, and a full 81% of parents fell in the normal range for stress three or more years post-disclosure.

Overall, we would make two observations about these findings. First, parents' emotional responses to their child's coming out—which often include heightened depression or anxiety—are not quickly resolved in

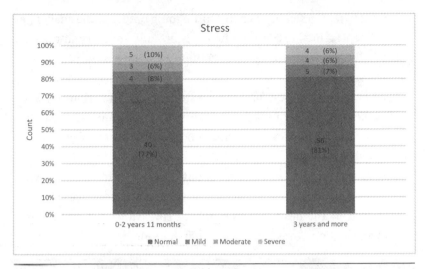

Figure 6.4. Comparison of parents with children who came out within three years (N=52) and parents with children who came out after three years or more (N=69) on measure of stress

most cases. While a significant percentage of parents soon after their child's disclosure will fall in the normal to mild range for depression (37% and 21%, respectively), anxiety (8% and 17%) and stress (77% and 8%), many others will struggle greatly after their child's disclosure, especially in the areas of depression and anxiety, and that struggle will often not be resolved quickly, possibly due to complicating circumstances.[10]

> *Parents' emotional responses to their child's coming out are not quickly resolved in most cases.*

Second, even after three or more years, the coming-out experience may well remain a challenge for many Christian parents. Again, while a significant proportion of parents fell in the normal range for depression, anxiety, and stress over time, some parents continued to struggle in important ways many years later, particularly in the area of anxiety.

These numbers illustrate a sobering reality, reflecting the initial and ongoing challenges parents face. We say this to normalize some of what you may be going through. If you find that you've been in a pretty difficult place and that you continue to struggle, you are not alone. It may be helpful to talk to someone about the ongoing nature of the challenges you've been facing. Those who hope to provide ministry and social support to Christian parents must commit to a long-term presence in their lives.

Ryan and Raegan, the couple whose story opened this chapter, faced grief as they came to terms with the reality of Remi's same-sex sexuality. Both Ryan and Raegan identified and processed their unspoken assumptions about how Remi's life—and their own lives—would now unfold. This grief was an *anticipatory grief* about a future different from what they had originally expected. Ryan and Raegan's experience of anticipatory grief fit the descriptions of both depression (dispirited, pessimistic) and anxiety (tense, easily upset, irritable).

> *Even losses that parents believe they have already grieved may wash over them afresh.*

Anticipatory grief can be diffuse and unfocused. It isn't just grieving one thing; it casts a wide net that catches many of parents' assumptions about how their child's life (and their own lives) will unfold. The disruption to parents' expectations—even when these expectations were not discussed but were taken for granted—can be a part of anticipatory grief. This kind of grief can also come in waves, at different life stages, when experiences that had been expected and are not occurring trigger new rounds of grief. For example, if a child who came out as a teen later marries a spouse of the same gender—or, conversely, if the child decides to remain celibate—parents might grieve over the opposite-sex marriage they had once imagined for their child. If a same-sex couple elects not to have children or has children through adoption, artificial insemination, or from a previous relationship, parents might grieve the absence of biological grandchildren (especially at a stage in life when their peers are becoming grandparents in this more traditional fashion). Even losses that parents believe they have already grieved may wash over them afresh at different life stages, causing them to question whether they have come to terms with their new reality.

Many parents find it helpful to name and process feelings such as anticipatory grief with a counselor, pastor, or trusted friend. Processing this grief in intentional settings can keep it from coming out "sideways" in less healthy ways, such as in exchanges with their child. Anticipatory grief is not the child's fault or responsibility; parents working through anticipatory grief find it important to maintain a boundary between themselves and their child, processing this grief on their own without manipulating their child.

In addition to anticipatory grief, many parents also experience a sense of fear about raising and relating to a gay child whose decisions about their own sexual identity and relationships may be unclear and whose lack of clarity can raise other concerns for parents. Fear-based parenting allows parents' fears and insecurities to take the lead in their decision-making. For example, the parent who attempts to control whether their son experiences same-sex attraction by cutting off all his contact with gay peers and supportive straight peers is parenting out of fear. Similarly, the parent who bans social media accounts, books, television, movies, music, and other entertainment with LGBTQ+ characters or sympathetic story lines in an attempt to prevent their daughter from being gay is parenting out of fear.

What could parents do instead? While precise approaches will be age-dependent, parents who recognize that their child is experiencing enduring same-sex attractions can use podcasts, television, movies, books, and other media depictions as opportunities to discuss what their child sees when they interact with this media. How does what they are seeing/reading/listening to reflect their own experience? What about this specific story drew them in? What did they like about it? What did they dislike?

Just as some parents have tried to cut off a child's contact with the outside world, some parents may try to control the words their child uses to name their experience. Parents might react negatively to words such as *gay*, *lesbian*, or *queer*, preferring person-first language that is more descriptive (for example, "I am a guy who experiences same-sex attraction"). But their child may prefer identity-first language (for example,

"I am queer"). Fear-based approaches to parenting might try to clamp down on a child's language preferences, rather than taking those preferences as an opportunity to understand their child better by recognizing that the child may be drawn to identity labels for a reason. This circumstance provides an opportunity to ask the child more about their language preferences and why those preferences exist. What draws them to the language they use? Have they always preferred that term, or was choosing between terms a journey for them too?

Fear-based approaches to parenting are not uncommon, particularly when parents face a crisis or perceived threat. Reducing fear-based parenting is a good sign that parents are laying healthy emotional foundations, reflecting their coming to terms with reality.

BARCLAY JONES, REFLECTING ON COMING TO TERMS WITH THE REALITY THAT HIS DAUGHTER EXPERIENCES SAME-SEX ATTRACTION

In my case it has not been a difficult reckoning. My daughter's lifestyle is one of celibacy, although I could come to terms with a committed relationship to another woman. I would rather see my child in a committed, loving relationship than seeing them live their life devoid of love or commitment. In the past I think people with same-sex attraction who committed to a lifestyle of celibacy often were monks, nuns, or priests. Living a celibate lifestyle in today's oversexualized society is considered very strange, but this has not always been the case.

Spiritual foundations. Like cognitive and emotional foundations, spiritual foundations play an important role in parents' coming to terms with reality. The experience of a child's coming out may have upended parents' beliefs about who God is and God's provision and promises. As parents come to terms with the reality of their child's same-sex sexuality, then, their thoughts and experiences of God will likely shift, even if their theological convictions remain the same. Facing circumstances that a person has no control over often causes that person to develop greater dependency on God. While every experience of parenting involves some loss of control, the unique challenges faced by families with a same-sex-oriented child can generate a heightened sense of things being out of parents' control. Though the path to dependency on God may move through experiences of spiritual drought—a sense that God is not present in parents' circumstances or is silent when they ask him to speak to them—this journey can lead in the long run to even greater spiritual stability.

For Ryan and Raegan, their family circumstances ultimately led them toward a greater dependency on God. But this path was fraught. They spent time in prayer and reading Scripture, but they had so many questions they couldn't find answers to. They did not feel supported by their local faith community. The advice they received from their associate pastor seemed full of oversimplifications, and when they followed that advice, it simply added fuel to the fire. This complicated their spiritual journey. The initial fantasy Raegan had, for instance, that Remi's same-sex sexuality would "go away" was vulnerable to their associate pastor's recommendation that Remi go to a parachurch ministry that sought to "heal" what it described as "sexual brokenness." Ryan and Raegan brought this plan up to Remi, leading to heightened conflict that lasted for weeks.

Not only was this parachurch organization's equation of heterosexuality with healing hurtful to Remi, but the fact that her parents didn't seem to be listening to her was deeply troubling. She had shared with them through tears about the many weeks she'd spent in her room asking God to take away her same-sex attractions, to no avail. Her parents' insistence on this ministry made Remi feel as though her parents had ignored her anguish, as though they thought she hadn't yet "brought her sexuality to the Lord." She had already shared with them that expecting God to change her sexual attractions had led to spiritual discouragement, and she was still recovering from that discouragement. Now she was angry with her parents and with her pastor for insisting that she return to a spiritually unhealthy mindset. Her parents, realizing that their pastor's advice had caused additional hurt, were now none too pleased either. The journey that ultimately led them to greater trust in God included grappling with the recognition that the advice of their church leaders could not always be trusted.

Parents who have come to terms with reality in relation to their spiritual foundations exhibit a greater capacity for trusting in God when they do not know or understand the future. Healthy spiritual foundations expand parents' capacity for hope that good will come of their circumstances. These foundations also inform how parents pray for wisdom, look at the big picture in order to move forward as a family, and exercise prudence in their day-to-day exchanges with one another, their child, their extended family, people in their local faith community, and others. Important spiritual questions may remain in parents' minds. They may continue to struggle with what their child's experience of sexuality means for their child's spiritual well-being. However, they can struggle thoughtfully with these questions because they have accepted the reality of their child's experience; they are no longer struggling from a place of denial or trying to minimize reality of the experience.

> *Healthy spiritual foundations expand parents' capacity for hope.*

It's not uncommon for parents to experience distance from God, anger toward God, confusion, or discouragement about the lack of helpful support or resources within their faith community. Spiritual growth and maturity are the work of the Spirit in the life of the parent over time, as they face circumstances that may seem impossible. The experience of God's faithfulness and sovereignty over circumstances lays a spiritual foundation for parents to accept the reality of their child's same-sex sexuality. These shifts prepare parents to walk with their child with greater peace and patience as God works out his purposes in their lives.

COMING TO TERMS WITH DIVERSE GENDER IDENTITIES

Whether kids come out as gay or transgender, parents have to make a mental adjustment in both cases about whom they understand their child to be. When a child comes out as gay, parents who previously assumed their child's attraction to the opposite sex have an adjustment to make. When a child comes out as transgender, however, parents are asked to make a more fundamental adjustment. One parent of a trans child recalled,

> I think I went into a period of mourning because the person you think your child is, is dead to you. I had a mental picture of [my son], who he was and what his future would look like, and suddenly that was gone. The future was completely unknown and completely different from anything I'd envisioned for the past fifteen years. I felt as if I'd been living in a lie in a way. I felt as if I didn't have anything to cling to.[a]

What does it mean to come to terms with your child's experience of a different gender identity from one that corresponds to their birth sex? The cognitive dimensions here are especially difficult because of what the parent is being asked to accept—that their child's experience of their gender has not been the experience likely assumed by the parents or by society. The question of how best to respond to atypical gender experiences is contested in society at large and even more contested in religious circles, where little substantive thought has gone into how to walk with people who share such experiences.

In our previous writing, we have discussed how different gender experiences may relate to a "looping effect," in which young people interact with the language and categories available to them for discussing gender and identity.[b] Because the available language has expanded dramatically, informed by the deconstruction of sex and gender norms, young people in particular are trying to figure out their gender and gender identity in ways that will likely be difficult for parents to understand or empathize with.

This dynamic makes coming to terms with reality that much more difficult. Parents face a number of important questions: Should their child be diagnosed with gender dysphoria? How will their child manage dysphoria if that is the diagnosis they receive? Is the child describing a transgender experience or an emerging gender identity such as gender nonbinary, gender expansive, bi-gender, or gender creative—and how is their teen defining and making sense of this identity? Is the teen searching for a way to meet other needs not directly related to gender and finding themselves drawn to the language and categories of diverse gender identities within the context of a larger search for identity and meaning?

Because of all these possibilities, coming to terms with reality will look different for different parents. Just as the cognitive dimensions of this journey often prove challenging, so too do the emotional dimensions. Empathy and compassion may come to the foreground for parents whose child is diagnosed with gender dysphoria, but other emotions—such as confusion, fear, and grief—are also common.

The spiritual foundations are made difficult in part because, as we noted above, few resources exist and little thought has been given to diverse experience of gender identity. This shortage of resources speaking into the experiences you and your child are facing can make it even more difficult to feel spiritually grounded.

Despite these challenges, we have found that parents are still able to benefit from coming to terms with the reality that their child is navigating an atypical experience of gender identity. Growing comfortable with language and adopting healthy habits of meaning making serve as a valuable starting point for future decisions and discernment, not only for parents but also for those in ministry and mental health professionals.

LYNN McDONALD ON COMING TO TERMS WITH THE REALITY OF HER SON'S SAME-SEX SEXUALITY

Coming to terms with the new normal felt more like surviving. My life went on relatively normal, except the thought of having a gay son was always in the back of my mind, haunting me. I did not want to have a gay son to be a part of my story, but I began to think, what if God did? Trusting God was the first step to my new norm and the beginning of hope and healing.

Coming to terms with reality is reflected in important shifts that occur over time. It is a movement from being more reactive to a place of greater stability. On one side of coming to terms with reality, parents struggle with wishful thinking and fear-based parenting; on the other side of coming to terms with reality, parents are in a much better position—in their thoughts, feelings, and faith—to enter into a more honest account of themselves, their child, and their circumstances. The ways in which their life has changed have now been given meaning, and they are positioned to have hope for God's future provision.

ADVICE FROM CHRISTIAN PARENTS

As you consider what it means to you to come to terms with the reality of your son or daughter being gay, there are pieces of advice that come from other Christian parents.

Entrusting your story to those who know you. The first piece of advice is to entrust your story to people who truly know you and know your child and your heart for one another. One mother shared about her experience finding people who she could process all of this with:

> I went to two friends who knew [daughter was gay], who knew me, knew [daughter], and knew the whole family. They are trusted and close with almost every one of our children. I finally called one of them and said to her, "I just need to talk about this. I don't know what to do with it. I don't know how to process it." That was tremendous. . . . We had a conversation about how hard it is to know how to deal with this.[11]

Keep a pace that is manageable for you. Sometimes it is our closest friends who also provide us with the boundaries we need to process where we are rather than mentally move toward the future and risk entering into fear-based parenting. A mother shared how she and her close friend would step back from that place of fear in their own conversations: "We would start to say, 'What does this mean for [daughter]'s future,' but we decided I couldn't do that. I couldn't go through all the things that I thought it meant."

Similarly, a father of a gay son shared, "Take one day as it come [*sic*]. Don't create problems for yourself in the future. Don't worry about a bridge that will come up four years from now. Don't create that problem today. There are plenty of things to deal with now."[12]

Keep a pace that is manageable to you. Entrust your story to those who can help you with that pace.

YOUR TURN: COMING TO TERMS WITH REALITY

Take some time at the end of this chapter to reflect on what it means to come to terms with the reality of your child's same-sex sexuality.

- How settled are you today about what you and your family are navigating?

- What questions or doubts do you have about your child's experiences of same-sex sexuality or gender identity?

- What are some practical ways you could explore those remaining questions? Who would be a good resource(s) for exploring those questions?

- Even though coming to terms with reality does not address all of the issues or concerns that may arise moving forward, if you have come to terms with this new normal, how does that help you today?

7

HOW THE CHURCH CAN HELP

Travis and Caroline sat down for a consultation and seemed absolutely defeated. Caroline said, "Thank you for meeting with us. We just haven't known where to go after trying so hard to talk with some of the leaders in our church. We were surprised—and kind of hurt, to be honest with you—when we seemed to hit a wall in those conversations." Caroline and Travis went on to share that when their son, Jackson, age seventeen, came out to them last fall, they scheduled a time to meet with their pastor and get some direction. According to Caroline, their pastor said, "It's sin. Let me start there. It's not the right thing for him, or anyone else for that matter, and his friends and our schools around here will likely push him and other kids more and more in that direction. But it isn't the right way, obviously, so we need to think together about how he got himself here and how he can get himself out." Caroline shared that the senior pastor apparently told the youth pastor about Jackson's sexuality without the approval of Jackson or his parents. The senior pastor instructed the youth pastor to "disciple Jackson around this issue" and "make sure the kids in the youth group understand that homosexuality is not going to be allowed in this church." As Caroline shared this story with us, she looked at her husband, then looked at us—we could see that, as she said it all out loud and watched our honest reaction, she was processing it all again. She shared that, looking back on that conversation with their pastor, his response didn't really make sense, but she couldn't put her finger on why. It made sense at the time. "Maybe you think we are bad parents

for even going along with this," she told us. "But we figured at the time
that he had met with other people like our son, and he was the pastor,
so we took him at his word that this was the best way to go. It sounds
crazy now."

In this concluding chapter, we want to explore how churches can support
Christian parents whose child comes out to them as gay. In other words,
how can pastors like the ones at Travis and Caroline's church do better
in coming alongside families with a gay child? While some families
might choose to leave their current church and go elsewhere after a child
comes out most Christian parents (about 60%, as we noted in chapter
five) do not change local churches after a child comes out to them as gay.[1]
While a significant percentage of parents do change churches (about
37%), most stay where they are. This means that even churches that do
not feel well equipped to respond to a child's coming out, or to support
parents responding to their child, will likely find themselves grappling
with these issues in a way that will permanently shape the families who
remain within them.

Families choose to remain in their churches, even when those
churches prove unhelpful, for a variety of reasons. For Travis and
Caroline, the decision to stay in their church, at least as of our meeting
with them, had to do it being their extended family's church, a tight-knit
community in a small town. Leaving the church would likely create more
gossip than staying. But staying in the church would also be difficult.
Travis and Caroline were considering ways to pull back somewhat from
the community without leaving. Maybe Jackson would not attend youth
group as often or at all; he didn't want to be there anyway. Maybe they
would just attend Sunday services but not other events for the time being.
They considered not going to any church: "Between leaving our home
church for another church in our small town or just not going to church,
we would probably just not go to church for a while," said Travis. "But we
are going to try to make it work somehow." As they left our offices, we
could tell that this was going to be a difficult decision for them, one that
had no easy answers moving forward.

Some parents will decide to go to another church. The other church might be gay affirming, or it might hold a traditional sexual ethic but be more supportive of their family.[2] What we want to do in this final chapter is offer a few reflections on how traditional churches could make changes to provide more meaningful support to Christian parents whose child is gay.

Our most recent research asked Christian parents of gay children what advice they had for churches interested in supporting families like theirs.[3] The rest of this chapter will explore many of their recommendations. These recommendations included lead with love, graciousness, and humility; "see us"; educate the body; and offer practical assistance (see fig. 7.1). Churches that improve in these ways have an opportunity to make the coming-out experience better all around: they can create a more loving church culture, one informed about sexuality and gender and aware that people in their faith community are navigating sexual and gender identity and faith. Recall that most parents stay in their church but are eager to see changes in how they and their family are supported by their church.

> **Churches have an opportunity to make the coming-out experience better all around.**

ADVICE FROM CHRISTIAN PARENTS

Lead with love, graciousness, and humility. We heard from Christian parents a desire to see churches lead more with love, graciousness, and humility, especially in relating to parents and gay kids. One parent offered, "I would so wish for someone from church to reach out to my child and tell them 'as expert' that God loves them." Similarly, another parent advised church leaders to offer encouragement in each family member's walk with God: "Accept and encourage each of us as the individual children of God that we are."

Churches will benefit parents and their children alike by being intentionally relational and intentionally formational.[4] When we talk about being intentionally relational, we mean that whether parents and their gay children have a positive or negative experience in a church will be based on the relationships they have with other members of that church community. As churches express what they believe doctrinally about sexuality and gender, it is important that doctrine not overshadow relationships. We noted previously that many Christian parents will begin to question some of their own beliefs about sexuality as they journey with their child. Churches would do well to journey with these parents through their questions rather than simply declaring stances from a relational distance. Churches will benefit from learning how to be in relationship even when beliefs about sexuality or gender are in tension.

We also heard parents discuss the importance of helping them and their child walk with God. This is what we mean by being "intentionally formational":[5] spiritual formation occurs in community, and a church can offer scaffolding for this spiritual formation through corporate worship, prayer, the reading of Scripture, and other spiritual practices (including spiritual retreats, fasting, and service). Some ministries make the mistake of focusing on getting people to "right" doctrine as a prerequisite to spiritual formation. Rather, we encourage churches to focus on growth in Christ with the expectation that the Holy Spirit will work in people's lives and provide guidance in the very areas church leaders may have concerns about. Spiritual formation is lifelong; it is important to help people cultivate their relationship with God through practices and in relationships sustained over time.

> *Spiritual formation occurs in community, and a church can offer scaffolding for this spiritual formation.*

Parents also stressed to us the idea of creating spiritually and emotionally safe environments in churches and youth groups. One parent shared her longing for "some level of assurance that my daughter is safe and accepted and won't be ostracized in any way."[6]

If you are a church leader, we want to stress to you the importance of creating intentionally secure environments.[7] That is, faith communities need to be emotionally and spiritually safe for people navigating challenging questions around sexuality, gender, and faith. The kind of spiritual formation that faith communities seek to encourage will be hindered if a person does not feel safe. To create a better environment, begin by identifying how the topics of sexual and gender identity create fears for people in your church, then find ways to address these fears. How Christians in leadership manage (or fail to manage) these fears can significantly affect the emotional and spiritual safety of others.

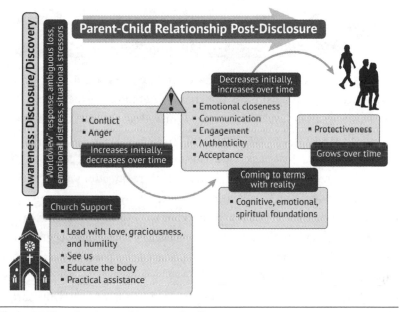

Figure 7.1. How churches could support families

Creating a safe environment for gay youth involves not only leaders' interactions directly with gay youth but also their work with other youth in youth ministry. Peers often shape climate in ways that can be difficult for youth navigating sexual or gender identity. For instance, if kids in a youth group are putting each other down by saying things such as "That's so gay" or "Stop acting so queer" as insults, this assumed disdain for LGBTQ+ people will make it that much more difficult for the person sorting out their own sexual or gender identity and faith.

Another practical recommendation parents made was for church leaders to check in regularly and often: "Approach us and ask how we are doing. Actually say, 'Let's get together and talk about your child and how you both are doing.' Not just once, but consistently. This doesn't go away."[8] Ministry in the realm of sexuality or gender identity is not conducted over a single meeting; it is a commitment to sustained relationship with a family. It means spending time with the youth, spending time with the parents, and maintaining those points of connection over several years.

> *Ministry in the realm of sexuality or gender identity*
> *is not conducted over a single meeting.*

Christian parents also longed for church leaders to exhibit humility in dealing with circumstances they hadn't personally experienced: "Be more curious than fundamental. Recognize that you don't understand and don't try to tell others what you think you know without having experienced it. Just ask questions with genuine curiosity for understanding."[9] It takes humility to ask sincere questions, to be curious rather than dogmatic. If navigating these challenges has not been a part of your own experience, demonstrate your willingness to learn.

We mentioned previously that parents are sometimes seen as the cause of a child's same-sex sexuality. Some of the parents we surveyed experienced this assumption from their church leaders, and they advised other leaders not to blame parents for a child being gay. One parent pleaded directly for "less certainty that I caused this."[10] For some leaders, letting go of this accusatory narrative will also require humility—specifically, the humility to admit all that is unknown about theories of causation and to resist the pull toward simplistic explanations that lay blame at the feet of parents or reduce a child's sexual attractions to "willful disobedience."

See us. Recent research in psychology has drawn our attention to the importance of micro-affirmations. Most people have heard of micro-aggressions, which are small indignities and slights directed toward another person. Micro-affirmations can be thought of as the opposite of micro-aggressions. They are small gestures or words that convey ideas such as, "I see you," "I believe you," and "You are valued here." One hope

Christian parents had for churches was that their church leaders and fellow church members would "see" them—that they would acknowledge and affirm their presence through micro-affirmations.

Many Christian parents reported not feeing seen in their churches. Once it became known that they had a gay child, parents often reported that others seemed to pull back from them. They felt isolated, like they were the topic of a conversation they were no longer a part of. Parents told us that it would have been helpful simply to hear others acknowledge their experience: "Sometimes we just need to hear that others recognize this is hard. And a true source of grief. We need to know others are interceding for the souls of our children."[11]

Parents also asked for those in ministry, especially youth ministry, to pursue relationship with gay kids: "I wish our youth pastor had been more engaged with the disengaged."[12]

One way to "see" people is to be open about the reality that a percentage of people experience same-sex attraction and are navigating questions of sexual and religious identity. One parent offered the following recommendation: "Openly acknowledge that Christians can experience same-sex attraction, so that it is not kept behind closed doors—but at the same time, promote surrender for all of us in our attractions to God's sexual ethic, trusting his ways are best."[13]

For this parent, acknowledging the existence of same-sex sexuality does not contradict with encouraging people to be obedient to a traditional sexual ethic. Instead, increased openness makes it possible for a church to promote sexual surrender for all people equally.

We cannot even discuss what it means for families with a gay child to thrive in their church if their church is a place where they must be largely closeted about their experience. One parent reflected: "Let us tell our stories openly to entire church—our problems and suffering don't need to be hidden. Others cannot find healing if we aren't allowed to share the healing & comfort we have found in Jesus and safe friends."[14]

Christian parents have described their desire to be seen, to be acknowledged as part of the body of Christ, to be cared about and cared for. "Seeing" a family in this way does not mean soliciting prayer requests about them as an excuse to gossip about their experience; prayers should be discreet and considerate. But we encourage church leaders to reach out to parents and check in with them. Let them know you care about them, that you don't think differently about them because they are navigating this experience with their child. Be sure to also express love for their child. If you already have a relationship with their child, reconnect with them to let them know how much they matter to you too. Don't pull back from the parents or the family; lean in, just as you might with any other family going through a difficult time and needing help to sort out difficult and complex spiritual questions. Stay engaged for the long term. The emotional challenges some parents face will extend for many years.

Educate the body. In our interviews, we had the sense that many traditional churches are not having conversations about sexuality even broadly speaking, let along conversations about the specific complexities of sexual or gender identity. One parent we surveyed advised churches to "talk, teach, educate the congregation on LGBT issues and sexuality in general."[15] What could this education focus on? Here are a few thoughts offered by parents: "Part of the education parents recommended has to do with recognizing that not everyone is straight and not everyone will marry." One parent advised churches to "have more sensitivity that not everyone will get married, not everyone is heterosexual. Talking like everyone is conforming to gender norms is hard to hear at times."[16]

Another part of education in a church setting simply involves discussing topics openly and listening to people within the community who have navigated these concerns: "Have the church truly talk about LGBTQ+ issues—hear those who struggle—talk to them, listen to them, hear their questions and hurts. Treat them as people with an identity that goes beyond just their sexual identity."[17]

Parents also expressed a desire for churches to state their beliefs with greater clarity, what one parent calls "an even clearer public articulation of who we are."[18] Since this simple statement can be layered with complexity, let's take a moment to unpack it.

Most people who are gay and affirming will want to know whether a church is gay affirming. At the same time, people who want to be a part of a church that adheres to a traditional Christian sexual ethic will want to know this information as well. Both groups want truth in advertising. Some churches that hold to a traditional Christian sexual ethic also desire to be missional to the LGBTQ+ community and to offer more nuanced ministry and support to families in this area. We recommend that such churches still be clear about their doctrinal positions, so that there is no bait and switch, in which a person is surprised after attending a church regularly for eight months to learn that the church is more traditional in its sexual ethic. At the same time, we agree that churches being traditional in their sexual ethic does not have to equate to churches being uncharitable, pushing a narrative of change to heterosexuality, or keeping people closeted.

Remember that parents want to be seen. They don't wish to be in hiding or to take a shame-based approach to their own family. Indeed, most of the parents we have surveyed were conservative but wanted their church to do better in caring for them as parents and for their child as a person navigating same-sex sexuality and faith. Positions such as these are challenging to explain in a web link. Churches should be prepared to be misunderstood, as most people around them may be unfamiliar with such nuance and want to move them toward a more black-and-white position. Even so, having clarity in doctrinal positions actually puts a church in a better position to explain its nuanced approach to ministry for missional purposes. In our experience, misunderstanding, hurt, and confusion often develop when churches are not clear about their doctrine but also try to be nuanced in ministry.

While education about the church's teachings on sexuality and gender will be important, these teachings are macro-level positions that will likely be read or heard in more stark terms as coming from a position of power. They will need to be balanced by a commitment to relationship, to valuing one another, and to reducing fear-based ways of leading and relating, so that people are able to recognize their value and worth to their community and to God.

Offer practical assistance. Practical assistance can take many forms. One recommendation parents made was for churches to offer a support group or specialized small group for families navigating sexual or gender identity. One parent, describing the value of a support group, explained, "Our small group has been supportive but doesn't really understand."[19] Many churches today use small groups as the first line of ministry for church members and regular attenders. Having parents plugged into this kind of a group can be a lifeline; it can be a truly valuable source of support to them. But some parents who have a child come out may benefit from a more specialized group that functions as a support group, in which several families could come together to share with and encourage one another.

A similar group could be offered to the gay family member. That person might benefit from meeting in a small group to study Scripture, pray, and be encouraged by others also trying to take their sexuality or gender seriously, take their faith as a follower of Christ seriously, and bring these two together meaningfully.

Groups specially designated to offer support have the added benefit of communicating to parents that they are not the only ones navigating this experience, and communicating to the gay family member that they are not the only gay person in the church. Such groups may be a step toward meeting one parent's appeal for "visible diversity within the church. I feel alone and as though we're the only ones dealing with this situation. My son feels that in a church of about 500 people he's the only gay person."[20] A smaller church may need to partner with other local churches to offer this kind of supportive group experience, but it could be well worth the effort to organize such a resource.

Another example of practical assistance is for churches to help cover the cost of Christian counseling for families in need. Many churches do have discretionary funds of some kind, but intentionally setting aside resources that could be allocated to such supportive services could demonstrate an even greater degree of attention and care.

Parents also expressed their desire for skilled pastoral counseling on these matters. Of course, the quality of pastoral care and counseling will be a reflection of many other considerations, but this is a practical need some parents identified.

Practical assistance could also take the form of equipping youth ministry staff to work with students who are attracted to the same sex. This is a far cry from the message Travis and Caroline's youth pastor received that "homosexuality is not going to be allowed in this church." Instead, churches and youth groups might choose to say, "We expect that a small percentage of people in our church experience same-sex attractions, and we want to be sure that they know they are loved by God and valued here. We want to walk alongside them as they face a number of decisions moving forward about how to make sense of their experience and what it looks like for them to trust God with this part of their lives."

Although few of the Christian parents we surveyed were in full-time ministry, those who were noted their desire for churches to provide resources to families like theirs: "The worst feeling for us was the sense of feeling alone. We are both ministers, and this has been a tough, lonely journey."[21] Those in ministry are sometimes the most isolated people in the church, and finding resources for them brings with it additional layers of complexity. A church already following some of the recommendations discussed above will be better positioned to support and not overreact to their own leadership if a leader's child shares their experiences of same-sex sexuality or navigating gender identity.

LYNN AND GREG McDONALD ON HOW THE CHURCH COULD SUPPORT FAMILIES WITH LGBTQ+ KIDS

Our recommendation for how churches can help families who have LGBTQ+ loved ones in their congregation and the community beyond their walls includes these principles:

1. Given that the majority of LGBTQ+ individuals leave their faith, we recommend being more concerned about reaching those outside your walls than keeping those inside your walls happy. Ministry is messy, and LGBTQ+ ministry is especially messy.

2. Be authentic. We all understand how seriously God takes sin. After all, God sacrificed his son so we all could be reconciled.

We can agree that we are new creations in God's sight when we acknowledge our sin, ask forgiveness, receive the gift of salvation, and follow Jesus to the best of our abilities. It's crucial to admit that the entire congregation is littered with sin from the pulpit on down: from gluttons to gossips, the angry, fornicators, people who view pornography regularly, the proud, idolators— and we haven't yet mentioned thieves, liars, and murderers. Even if you believe being LGBTQ+ is sinful, be cautious not to be hypocritical toward LGBTQ+ individuals. It will push them further away from God.

3. Be committed to make your church the safest place for any child, youth, or adult to wrestle with their spirituality, sexuality, gender identity, drug addiction, or anything else.

4. Start a parent support group for parents with LGBTQ+ children (even if it has to be virtual). Recognize that you have plenty of LGBTQ+ individuals and their loved ones in your congregation whether you know it or not. . . . Families with LGBTQ+ children are starving for the local church to help them on this journey without judgment. We know firsthand from walking one-on-one with over a thousand Christian parents who have LGBTQ+ loved ones that when Mom and Dad get healthy, the child gets healthy. Both grow in a deeper relationship with each other and God.

5. Be good listeners. Hear their story and respond in love and compassion, not feeling like you have to judge or fix it for them.

6. Be open to getting educated by reading books on the subject from both sides. It is important to understand that scientific study is revealing new data and learnings.

HOW THE CHURCH COULD SUPPORT PARENTS WITH TRANSGENDER CHILDREN

Many of the recommendations offered in this chapter will also apply to churches wanting to support families navigating diverse gender identities. Leading with love, graciousness, and humility is crucial for churches supporting these families. So too is making sure that parents and their child are seen, that people check in with them and maintain relationships of depth and substance. Creating space for difficult questions to be raised, and learning to sit in the tensions sparked by those questions, will be of great value to every family.

While educating the church remains important for supporting families navigating gender identity, the most vital type of education to support these families will have a different focus from education centered on experiences of attraction to the same sex. Education should instead focus on understanding dysphoria and diverse gender identities, and strategies for using language in a way that honors people whose internal sense of gender is in process. In addition, it may be helpful to discuss changes in the larger society's conceptualization of sex and gender, as well as how the church is positioning itself alongside those conversations.[a] We recommend demonstrating intellectual humility about what can and cannot be known from Scripture, science, and personal experience, especially in cases where people's experiences seem to be in tension with the church's understanding of Scripture.

For transgender persons in the church, Christian parents also identified the practical need to address bathroom use—they recommended making family bathrooms or single-stall bathrooms available so that the question of which bathroom to use could become less of an issue.

It is essential to express your commitment to journeying with a family whose child is sorting out gender identity. The parents and their child will likely face difficult decisions in the days ahead about gender identity, expression, and managing gender dysphoria in cases where dysphoria is present. Parents are often encouraged to know that their faith community has worked to gain a better grasp of what their experience is like and some of the challenges and decisions they may face.

CONCLUSION

Many of our parents don't trust churches and have been hurt by their church. Yet most stay in their home church. They want their church to change in some meaningful way.[22]

The recommendations in this chapter represent ways Christian parents are asking the church to become a local faith community that families will want to remain a part of. In agreement with these parents, we encourage you not to be reactive to a person coming out but to instead be proactive in shaping your church climate now, under the assumption that there are already people in the church navigating sexual and gender identity questions.

> *Be proactive in shaping your church climate now.*

The kind of church these families would want to remain a part of is a church where there was no shame in having a child experience same-sex sexuality or gender dysphoria. Same-sex sexuality and diverse gender experiences are a reality for a percentage of the population. The more churches can adjust to that reality and prepare to be a resource to those who are already a part of the body of Christ, the better off each family will be.

To become the kind of church that a family would want to remain a part of, think about what is already being shared in your faith community and how your people respond to real-life challenges. If a church does not have a track record of rising to the occasion and caring well for one another in other areas of concern, they are not likely to be helpful in these complicated areas of care for one another. If your church has a good reputation in other areas of rising to the occasion, of meeting people where they are without shaming them, then the church is in a better position to pivot those resources and ways of relating toward this experience as well. Though it will require additional education and exposure to people navigating these concerns, your church has the opportunity to shift toward greater love, support, humility, graciousness, and awareness.

YOUR TURN: HOW YOUR CHURCH COULD SUPPORT YOU

If you are a parent of an LGBTQ+ child, take some time at the end of this chapter to reflect on specific ways your church could be more of a support to you and your family. If you are a church leader, consider how parents within your congregation might answer these questions.

- How would you describe the support you and your family have received from your church so far?

- Take a blank sheet of paper and draw a line down the middle. Write "helpful" on one side of the line and "unhelpful" on the other. List specific things have been helpful and jot down why they were helpful to you or your child. What has been unhelpful? Jot those things down, as well as what made them unhelpful.

- Based on what you have read in this chapter and the recommendations from other Christian parents, what else would you add to the list of potentially helpful things your church could do? What makes those things helpful to you or your child? Whom could you talk to in your church about the things you believe could be helpful (and why)?

NOTES

WHAT THIS BOOK IS ABOUT AND WHY IT MATTERS, OR WHO WE ARE AND HOW TO READ THIS BOOK

[1]Maslowe & Yarhouse, 2015. The larger project is reported in Maslowe, 2012.

[2]Cruise et al., 2021.

[3]Biondolillo et al., 2021.

[4]Indeed, the average time parents were interviewed after their son or daughter came out was approximately four years for data from the study of two hundred Christian parents and approximately five years for the 125 Christian parents from our most recent survey. See Cruise et al., 2021.

1. HOW PARENTS BECOME AWARE

[1]Aranda et al., 2015.

[2]See, e.g., D'Amico et al., 2015, 411; Maguen et al., 2002.

[3]Reed et al., 2020.

[4]Cruise et al., 2021.

[5]Rosario, Schrimshaw, & Hunter, 2004.

[6]Ben-Ari, 1995; Strommen, 1989; Freedman, 2008; Saltzburg, 2004; D'Augelli et al., 1998.

[7]D'Augelli et al., 1998; Savin-Williams, 2001; Savin-Williams & Dube, 1998.

[8]See, e.g., D'Augelli et al., 1998.

[9]Reed et al., 2020.

[10]Reed et al. 2020, 46.

[11]Erspamer, 2013.

[12]Cramer & Roach, 1988; Freedman, 2008; Merighi & Grimes, 2000; Robinson et al., 1989; Savin-Williams & Dube, 1998.

[13]Savin-Williams & Dube, 1998.

[14]Maslowe & Yarhouse, 2015.

[15]Our major studies of Christian parents do not reflect significant racial diversity. For example, in our most recent survey of 125 Christian parents, 95% identified as European American, 1.6% as African American, and 1.6% as Hispanic/Latino. Similarly, Sides reported on the demographic characteristics from the Marin Foundation project—the study of 200 Christian parents—and 94.6% were Caucasian, 4% Hispanic, 2% identified as mixed race, and 1% Asian American.

[16]Savin-Williams & Dube, 1998; Ben-Ari, 1995.

[17]Ben-Ari, 1995.

[18]Maslowe & Yarhouse, 2015.

[19]Maslowe, 2012, 72; Ben-Ari, 1995.

[20]Zaporozhets et al., 2015.

[21]Zaporozhets et al., 2015.

[22]Cruise et al., 2021.

[23]Zaporozhets et al., 2015.

[24]Zaporozhets et al., 2015.

[25]Zaporozhets et al., 2015.

[26]Zaporozhets et al., 2015.

[27]Cruise et al., 2021.

[28]Zaporozhets et al., 2015.

[29]Zaporozhets et al., 2015.

[30]Zaporozhets et al., 2015.

[31]Zaporozhets et al., 2015.

[32]Zaporozhets et al., 2015.

[33]Yarhouse, et al., *2018.*

[34]Zaporozhets et al., 2015.

[35]Authors' files, The Marin Foundation (TMF).

[36]Authors' files, TMF.

[37]Authors' files, TMF.

[38]Authors' files, TMF.

[39]Authors' files, TMF.

[40]Authors' files.

[41]Zaporozhets et al., 2015.

[42]Zaporozhets et al., 2015.

[43]Zaporozhets et al., 2015.

[44]Zaporozhets et al., 2015.

[45]Zaporozhets et al., 2015.

[46]Zaporozhets et al., 2015.

[47] Authors' files.

[48] Authors' files.

[49] Authors' files.

[50] Authors' files.

[51] Authors' files.

[52] Authors' files.

[53] See Yarhouse, 2019.

[54] Yarhouse, 2019.

[55] Biondolillo et al., 2021.

[56] Biondolillo et al., 2021.

[57] Biondolillo et al., 2021.

[58] Allen, 2018.

[59] Allen, 2018, 49.

[60] Allen, 2018, 49.

[61] Allen, 2018, 50.

[62] Allen, 2018, 56.

2. HOW PARENTS SEEK HELP

[1] Maslowe & Yarhouse, 2015.

[2] Chrisler, 2017.

[3] Johnson & Yarhouse, 2013.

[4] See Yarhouse, 2010, 57-80.

[5] Kramer et al., 2002.

[6] Sung et al., 2015.

[7] Maslowe & Yarhouse, 2015.

[8] Allen, 2018, 52.

[9] Allen, 2018, 52.

[10] Allen, 2018, 52.

[11] Allen, 2018, 57.

[12] Allen, 2018, 55.

[13] Allen, 2018, 55.

[14] Zaporozhets, Lane, et al., 2014; Zaporozhets, Campbell, et al., August 2014; Zaporozhets et al., 2015.

[15] In our previous study of ex-gay ministries, we found that people who were a part of these ministries reported benefits from having a parachurch ministry to be a part of, a space for prayer, study of Scripture, fellowship, and corporate worship. Similarly, the American Psychological Association's 2009 task force report on *appropriate therapeutic responses to sexual orientation* noted that, while there did not appear to be sufficient evidence to support

the claim that sexual orientation changed as a result of participating in such ministries, participants reported benefits from the social support found therein. See Jones & Yarhouse, 2007.

3. HOW PARENTS MAINTAIN THE RELATIONSHIP

[1]We worked with this family for some time and discuss their story in greater detail in Yarhouse 2019, 227-33. The interested reader will want to review that case for more of the nuances that go into case conceptualization and treatment planning.

[2]Maslowe & Yarhouse, 2015.

[3]Maslowe & Yarhouse, 2015.

[4]Authors' files.

[5]Authors' files.

[6]Ibid., 50.

[7]Authors' files.

[8]Authors' files.

[9]Authors' files.

[10]Zaporozhets et al., 2015.

[11]Zaporozhets et al., 2015.

[12]Authors' files.

[13]Authors' files.

[14]Authors' files.

[15]Caitlyn Ryan has shown through her research at *the Family Acceptance Project* that parents' accepting and rejecting behaviors have a significant impact on their child who has come out to them. Rejecting behaviors put the child at great risk for things such as attempted suicide, significant depression, illegal drug use, and more. These rejecting behaviors include hitting, slapping, physical injury, verbal harassment, excluding them from family activities, and blaming the child if they were to experience harassment. Accepting behaviors are behaviors that will likely help a child, such as supporting their LGBTQ+ identity, advocating for them, finding adult role models, and bringing them to LGBTQ+ events. Some of these behaviors might not be as readily achievable for conservative Christian parents who experience value conflicts. In terms of a young person's safety and well-being, adopting accepting behaviors is not as critical as avoiding rejecting behaviors, but even small shifts can make a big difference. See Ryan, 2009.

[16]Zaporozhets et al., 2015.

[17]Zaporozhets et al., 2015.

[18]Zaporozhets et al., 2015.
[19]Zaporozhets et al., 2015.
[20]Allen, 2018.
[21]Allen, 2018, 50.
[22]Allen, 2018, 53.
[23]Allen, 2018, 53.
[24]Allen, 2018, 51.
[25]Allen, 2018, 51.
[26]Authors' files; Campbell et al., 2015.

4. HOW THE PARENT-CHILD RELATIONSHIP CHANGES

[1]Campbell, 2015.
[2]Campbell, 2015.
[3]Campbell, 2015.
[4]These themes are derived primarily from qualitative analysis. However, in our recent survey of 125 Christian parents, we examined the question of changes quantitatively and found support for the qualitative analysis. For example, here are three tables showing statistically significant changes in closeness, engagement, authenticity, and other relationship qualities before coming out (table 4.1), at the time of coming out (table 4.2), and at the time of the interview (table 4.3).

Table 4.1. Relationship before coming out

Quality	Low 0-25% of the time		Somewhat 26-50% of the time		Moderate 51-76% of the time		High 76-100% of the time	
	n	%	n	%	n	%	n	%
Closeness	5	4.3	17	14.5	37	31.6	58[a]	49.6
Engaged	6	4.9	15	12.4	46	38.0	54	44.6
Authentic	4	3.4	14	11.9	37	31.6	62	52.9
Accepting	1	0.9	12	10.2	30	25.4	75[ac]	63.6
Supporting	2	1.7	6	5.0	26	21.9	85[ac]	71.4
Argumentative	70	60.9	23	20.0	16	13.9	6	5.2

Note: a = significant shift between high category and all the rest for tables 4.1 and 4.2;
b = significant shift between high category and all the rest for tables 4.2 and 4.3;
c = significant shift between high category and all the rest for tables 4.1 and 4.3.

Table 4.2. Relationship at the time of coming out

Quality	Low 0-25% of the time		Somewhat 26-50% of the time		Moderate 51-76% of the time		High 76-100% of the time	
	n	%	n	%	n	%	n	%
Closeness	17	14.7	15	12.9	42	36.2	42[a]	36.2
Engaged	19	16.1	13	11.0	41	34.8	45	38.1
Authentic	9	7.6	21	17.7	34	28.6	55	46.2
Accepting	13	10.9	18	15.1	43	36.1	45[ab]	37.8
Supporting	12	10.3	15	12.8	39	33.3	51[ab]	43.6
Argumentative	65	55.6	25	21.4	15	12.8	12[b]	10.3

Table 4.3. Relationship at the time of the interview (now)

Quality	Low 0-25% of the time		Somewhat 26-50% of the time		Moderate 51-76% of the time		High 76-100% of the time	
	n	%	n	%	n	%	n	%
Closeness	16	13.6	13	11.0	37	31.4	52	44.1
Engaged	15	12.6	16	13.5	43	36.1	45	37.8
Authentic	11	9.3	10	8.5	34	28.8	63	53.4
Accepting	8	6.8	11	9.4	40	34.2	58[bc]	49.6
Supporting	4	3.4	10	8.5	33	27.9	71[bc]	60.2
Argumentative	78	69.0	21	18.6	11	9.7	3[b]	2.7

[5] Houp, 2018, 85.
[6] Authors' files.
[7] Campbell, 2015, 62.
[8] Authors' files.
[9] Authors' files.
[10] Houp, 2018, 86.
[11] Campbell et al., 2017, 336-44.
[12] Houp, 2018, 75-76.
[13] Houp, 2018, 76.
[14] Authors' files.
[15] Campbell, 2015, 56.
[16] Houp, 2018.
[17] Campbell et al., 2017, 336-44.
[18] Campbell, 2015, 58.

[19]Houp, 2018, 79.
[20]Houp, 2018, 80.
[21]Campbell et al., 2015.
[22]Houp, 2018, 81.
[23]Campbell, 2015, 59.
[24]Campbell, 2015, 60.
[25]Houp, 2018, 84.
[26]Authors' files.
[27]Campbell et al., 2017, 336-44.
[28]Houp, 2018, 87.
[29]Houp, 2018, 87.
[30]Houp, 2018, 87.
[31]Campbell, 2015, 63.
[32]Campbell, 2015, 63.
[33]Yarhouse et al., 2016, 66.
[34]See Houp, 2018.
[35]Houp, 2018.
[36]Reed et al., 2020.
[37]Houp, 2018.
[38]Houp, 2018.
[39]Houp, 2018, 60-61.
[40]Houp, 2018, 64.
[41]Houp, 2018, 65.
[42]Houp, 2018, 66.
[43]Houp, 2018, 66

5. HOW FAITH CHANGES

[1]There would be greater commitment to the view that same-sex behavior is sin and more variability on the claim that experiencing same-sex attraction is itself sin.
[2]We saw this, too, in our most recent survey, in which 63% of parents indicated that during the process of coming out, they were relying on God's sovereignty as a source of comfort.
[3]Campbell, 2015, 73.
[4]Houp, 2018.
[5]Authors' files.
[6]Authors' files.
[7]Aleteia, 2016.
[8]Houp, 2018, 102-3.

[9]Allen, 2018.

[10]Allen, 2018.

[11]Campbell, 2015, 76.

[12]Houp, 2018, 100-101.

[13]Houp, 2018, 101.

[14]Allen, 2018, 52.

[15]Authors' files.

[16]Houp, 2018, 103.

[17]See Pargament, 1997.

[18]Erspamer, 2013.

[19]Our most recent sample of Christian parents scored high on a measure of religiosity, the DUREL, which looks at organizational religiosity (frequency of church or related meeting attendance), nonorganizational religiosity (frequency of time spent in religious activities, such as prayer and Bible study), and intrinsic religiosity (carrying religion into all aspects of life). Our sample scored high on all three of these dimensions of religiosity.

[20]Houp, 2018, 94.

[21]Campbell, 2015, 72; see also Campbell et al., 2015.

[22]Campbell, 2015, 71.

[23]Campbell, 2015, 71.

[24]Houp, 2018, 94.

[25]Houp, 2018, 95.

[26]Campbell, 2015, 72.

[27]Sides, 2017; Sides et al., 2017; see also Zaporozhets et al., 2015.

[28]Sides, 2017, 57.

[29]Sides, 2017, 57.

[30]Sides, 2017, 57.

[31]Sides, 2017, 57.

[32]Authors' files.

[33]Sides, 2017, 60.

[34]Sides, 2017, 60.

[35]Sides, 2017, 60.

[36]Sides, 2017, 65.

[37]Sides, 2017, 60.

[38]Sides, 2017, 60.

[39]Sides, 2017, 58.

[40]Sides, 2017, 59.

[41]Sides, 2017, 59.

[42]Sides, 2017, 61.
[43]Sides, 2017, 61.
[44]Authors' files.
[45]Sides, 2017, 62.
[46]Sides, 2017, 63.
[47]Sides, 2017, 64.
[48]Sides, 2017, 71.
[49]Sides, 2017, 71.
[50]Sides, 2017, 72.
[51]Sides, 2017, 77.
[52]Sides, 2017, 77.
[53]Sides, 2017, 78.
[54]Sides, 2017, 81.
[55]Sides, 2017, 72.
[56]Sides, 2017, 84.
[57]Sides, 2017, 75.
[58]Authors' files.
[59]Allen, 2018, p. 57.

6. HOW PARENTS COME TO TERMS WITH REALITY

[1]Ben-Ari's (1995) study made a distinction between acknowledgment and acceptance. Acknowledgment was "recognition of a fact" (107); acceptance "included an affective component" (107). Ben-Ari offers, "One can acknowledge a fact without accepting it, but not vice versa. In that respect, acknowledgment is a pre-condition for acceptance" (107). Acceptance in this study seemed to have an affirmational quality, although this quality is not stated overtly. For Christian parents, coming to terms with reality seems to be primarily concerned with acknowledgment. Acceptance in this case may indeed be a precondition to parents being as affirmative as possible of child within the parent's Christian beliefs, values, and remaining spiritual questions.

[2]Maslowe & Yarhouse, 2015.

[3]See Park, 2005, 707-29.

[4]In Ben-Ari's (1995) study, the most common motivation for disclosure was not wanting to hide, not wanting to live a lie—something identified by both gay children and their parents.

[5]https://betterworldhealthcare.com/depression-anxiety-stress-scales -short-form-dass-21/. For more information, see Lovibond & Lovibond (1995).

[6]Psychology Foundation of Australia, 2018.

[7]Psychology Foundation of Australia, 2018.

[8]Psychology Foundation of Australia, 2018.

[9]Here are our findings on depression, anxiety, and stress by severity *within* three years of coming out:

Table 6.1.

Severity Rating	Depression		Anxiety		Stress	
	n	Percent	n	Percent	n	Percent
Normal	19	37	4	8	40	77
Mild	11	21	9	17	4	8
Moderate	13	25	7	13	3	6
Severe/ Extremely Severe	9	17	32	62	5	10

Here are our findings on depression, anxiety, and stress by severity *after* three years of coming out:

Table 6.2.

Severity Rating	Depression		Anxiety		Stress	
	n	Percent	n	Percent	n	Percent
Normal	23	33	15	22	56	81
Mild	25	36	10	14	5	7
Moderate	16	23	18	26	4	6
Severe/ Extremely Severe	5	7	26	38	4	6

We also compared parents of LGBTQ+ children and parents of transgender children but found no significant differences between these groups on the DASS-21.

[10]It should be noted that because we do not have comparison data from these parents from before their child came out, we cannot definitively say whether their emotions are affected most by their child's sexuality or by other factors in their lives.

[11]Authors' files.

[12]Authors' files.

7. HOW THE CHURCH CAN HELP

[1]Sides, 2017.

[2]Sides, 2017.

[3]Cruise et al., 2021.
[4]Yarhouse et al., 2018.
[5]Yarhouse et al., 2018.
[6]Cruise et al., 2021.
[7]Yarhouse et al., 2018.
[8]Cruise et al., 2021.
[9]Cruise et al., 2021.
[10]Cruise et al., 2021.
[11]Cruise et al., 2021.
[12]Cruise et al., 2021.
[13]Cruise et al., 2021.
[14]Cruise et al., 2021.
[15]Cruise et al., 2021.
[16]Cruise et al., 2021.
[17]Cruise et al., 2021.
[18]Cruise et al., 2021.
[19]Cruise et al., 2021.
[20]Cruise et al., 2021.
[21]Cruise et al., 2021.
[22]In our most recent survey of 125 Christian parents, 80% reported staying in their church, and 70% wanted the church to change in some meaningful way to be more supportive of them and their family.

SIDEBAR NOTES

1. HOW PARENTS BECOME AWARE
[a]Yarhouse et al., 2016.
[b]Yarhouse et al., 2016.

2. HOW PARENTS SEEK HELP
[a]Yarhouse et al., 2016.

3. HOW PARENTS MAINTAIN THE RELATIONSHIP
[a]Yarhouse et al., 2016.
[b]Yarhouse et al., 2016.
[c]Authors' files. TMF
[d]Zaporozhets et al., 2015, or Author's files

4. HOW THE PARENT-CHILD RELATIONSHIP CHANGES
[a]Yarhouse et al., 2016.

5. HOW FAITH CHANGES
[a]Yarhouse et al., 2016.

6. HOW PARENTS COME TO TERMS WITH REALITY
[a]Zaporozhets et al., 2014.
[b]Yarhouse & Sadusky, 2020.

7. HOW THE CHURCH CAN HELP
[a]Yarhouse & Sadusky, 2020.

REFERENCES

Aleteia. (2016, August 15). Blessed Mother Teresa teaches us how to find "oneness with God." https://aleteia.org/2016/08/15/watch-blessed-mother-teresa-teaches-us-how-to-find-oneness-with-god/

Allen, A. (2018). Advice of Christian parents to parents and LGBT children during disclosure (Publication No. 13425429) [Doctoral dissertation, Regent University]. ProQuest Dissertations & Theses Global.

Aranda, F., Matthews, A. K., Hughes, T. L., Muramatsu, N., Willsnack, S. C., Johnson, T. P., & Riley, B. B. (2015). Coming out in color: Racial/ethnic differences in relationship between level of sexual identity disclosure and depression among lesbians. *Cultural Diversity and Ethnic Minority Psychology, 21*(2), 247-57.

Ben-Ari, A. (1995). The discovery that an offspring is gay: Parents,' gay men's, and lesbian's perspectives. *Journal of Homosexuality, 30*, 89-112.

Biondolillo, K., Hardyman, M., Martin, E., Seibert, A., Amitrano, N., Newcomer, A., Zaporozhets, O., & Yarhouse, M. A. (2021, March 25). *How the church can support sexual minorities and their families: A survey of LGBTQ+ persons who came out to Christian parents* [Poster presentation]. Christian Association for Psychological Studies National Conference.

Campbell, M. C. (2015). *Changes in parent-child relationships and religious views in parents of LGB youth post-disclosure* (Publication No. 3730351) [Doctoral dissertation, Regent University]. ProQuest Dissertations & Theses Global.

Campbell, M. C., Yarhouse, M. A., Zaporozhets, O., Hamilton, A., Houp, D., Statesir, L., & Marin, A. (2015, April). [Poster presentation]. Christian Association for Psychological Studies National Conference, Denver.

Campbell, M. C., Zaporozhets, O., & Yarhouse, M. A. (2017). Change in parent-child relationships and religious views in parents of LGB youth post-disclosure. *The Family Journal, 25*(4), 336-44.

Chrisler, A. J. (2017). Understanding parent reactions to coming out as lesbian, gay, or bisexual: A theoretical framework. *Journal of Family Theory & Review, 9*, 165-81.

Cramer D. W., & Roach, A. J. (1988). Coming out to mom and dad: A study of gay males and their relationships with their parents. *Journal of Homosexuality, 15*, 79-91.

Cruise, C., Lewis, A., Amitrano, N., McRay, M., Haarer, M., Yarhouse, J., & Zaporozhets, O. (2021, March 25). *Parents of LGBTQ+ loved ones speak to their churches* [Poster presentation]. Christian Association for Psychological Studies National Conference.

D'Amico, E., Julien, D., Tremblay, N., & Chartrand, E. (2015). Gay, lesbian, and bisexual youths coming out to their parents: Parental reactions and youths' outcomes. *Journal of GLBT Family Studies, 11*(5), 411.

D'Augelli, A. R., Hershberger, S. L., & Pilkington, N. W. (1998). Lesbian, gay, and bisexual youth and their families: Disclosure of sexual orientation and its consequences. *American Journal of Orthopsychiatry, 68*(3), 361-71.

Erspamer, T. (2013). *Reactions in parents of gay, lesbian, and bisexual children* (Publication No. 3574085) [Doctoral dissertation, Regent University]. UMI Dissertation publishing.

Freedman, L. (2008). Accepting the unacceptable: Religious parents and adult gay and lesbian children. *Families in Society: The Journal of Contemporary Social Services, 89*(2), 237-44.

Houp, Dara R. (2018). *The role of contact on parent-child relationships and religious views in parents of LGB youth* (Publication No. 10846639) [Doctoral dissertation, Regent University]. ProQuest Dissertations & Theses Global.

Johnson, V. R. F., & Yarhouse, M. A. (2013). Shame in sexual minorities: Stigma, internal cognitions, and counseling considerations. *Counseling and Values, 58*, 85-103.

Jones, S. L., & Yarhouse, M. A. (2007). *Ex-gays? A longitudinal study of religiously mediated change in sexual orientation.* InterVarsity Press.

Kramer, E. J., Kwong, K., Lee, E., & Chung, H. (2002). Cultural factors influencing the mental health of Asian Americans. *Western Journal of Medicine, 176*(4), 227-31.

Lovibond, S. H. & Lovibond, P. F. (1995). *Manual for the Depression Anxiety Stress Scales.* (2nd. Ed.) Psychology Foundation.

Maguen, S., Floyd, F. J., Bakeman, R., & Armistead, L. (2002). Developmental milestones and disclosure of sexual orientation among gay, lesbian, and bisexual youths. *Journal of Applied Developmental Psychology*, *23*(2), 219-33.

Maslowe, K. E. (2012). *Christian parental responses to their child's disclosure of experiences of same-sex attraction* (Publication No. 3528142) [Doctoral dissertation, Regent University]. UMI Dissertation publishing.

Maslowe, K. E., & Yarhouse, M. A. (2015). Christian parental reactions when a LGB child comes out. *American Journal of Family Therapy, 43*(4), 1-12.

Merighi, J. R., & Grimes, M. D. (2000). Coming out to families in a multicultural context. *Families in Society: The Journal of Contemporary Social Services, 81*(1), 32-41.

Pargament, K. (1997). *The psychology of religion and coping: Theory, research, and practice.* Guilford Press.

Park, C. L. (2005). Religion as a meaning-making framework for coping with life stress. *Journal of Social Issues, 61*(4), 707-29.

Psychology Foundation of Australia. (2018, July 26). Overview of the DASS and its uses. *Depression Anxiety Stress Scales (DASS).* http://www2.psy .unsw.edu.au/dass/over.htm

Reed, J., Stratton, S. P., Koprowski, G., Dillon, C., Dean, J. B., Yarhouse, M. A., Lastoria, M., & Bucher, E. (2020). "Coming out" to parents in a Christian context: A consensual qualitative analysis of LGB student experiences. *Counseling and Values, 65*, 38-56.

Robinson, B. E., Walters, L. H., & Skeen, P. (1989). Responses of parents to learning that their child is homosexual and concern over AIDS: A national study. *Journal of Homosexuality, 18*, 59-80.

Rosario, M., Schrimshaw, E., & Hunter, J. (2004). Ethnic/racial differences in the coming-out process of lesbian, gay, and bisexual youths: A comparison of sexual identity development over time. *Cultural Diversity and Ethnic Minority Psychology, 10*(3), 215-28.

Ryan, Caitlyn. (2009). *Supportive families, healthy children: Helping families with lesbian, gay, bisexual & transgender children.* Family Acceptance Project, Marian Wright Edelman Institute, San Francisco State University.

Saltzburg, S. (2004). Learning that an adolescent child is gay or lesbian: The parent experience. *Social Work, 49*(1), 109-18.

Savin-Williams, R. C. (2001). *Mom, dad. I'm gay. How families negotiate coming out.* American Psychological Association.

Savin-Williams, R. C., & Dube, E. M. (1998). Parental reactions to their child's disclosure of a gay/lesbian identity. *Family relations, 47*(1), 7-13.

Sides, J. D. (2017). Religious support for parents of children who have come out as lesbian, gay, or bisexual (Publication No. 10260025) [Doctoral dissertation, Regent University]. ProQuest Dissertations & Theses Global.

Sides, J. D., Yarhouse, M. A., Zaporozhets, O., Hamilton, A., Houp, D., Sadusky, J., Statesir, L., & Marin, A. (2017, August). *Meaning-making among parents when a child comes out* [Poster presentation]. National Convention of the American Psychological Association, Washington, DC.

Strommen, E. (1989). You're a what? Family member reactions to the disclosure of homosexuality. *Journal of Homosexuality, 18*, 37-58.

Sung, M. R., Szymanski, D. M., & Henrichs-Beck, C. (2015). Challenges, coping, and benefits of being an Asian American lesbian or bisexual woman. *Psychology of Sexual Orientation and Gender Diversity, 2*(1), 52-64. www.workcover.wa.gov.au/wp-content/uploads/sites/2/2015/07/3 .dass21withscoringinfo.pdf.

Yarhouse, M. A. (2010). *Homosexuality and the Christian*. BethanyHouse.

Yarhouse, M. A. (2019). *Sexual Identity and Faith: Helping Clients Achieve Congruence*. Templeton Press.

Yarhouse, M. A., Dean, J. B., Stratton, S. P., & Lastoria, M. (2018). *Listening to sexual minorities: A study of faith and sexuality on Christian college campuses*. IVP Academic, 2018.

Yarhouse, M. A., Houp, D., Sadusky, J., Zaporozhets, O., Statesir, L., & Marin, A. (2016, August). The meaning and experience of Christian parents when transgender children come out. In M. Brennan-Ing & E. L. Deneke (Cochairs), *The Intersection of Transgender and Gender Nonconforming Identities, Religion, and Spirituality* [Symposium] Annual Convention of the American Psychological Association, Denver.

Yarhouse, M. A., & Sadusky, J. (2020). *Emerging gender identities*. Brazos.

Zaporozhets, O., Campbell, M. C., Bucher, E., Yarhouse, M. A., Silander, N., Leary, A., Lane, C., Sides, J., Statesir, L., & Marin, A. (2014, August). *What are helpful and unhelpful resources to Christian parents when a gay child comes out?* [Poster presentation]. American Psychological Association National Convention, Washington, DC.

Zaporozhets, O., Lane, C., Campbell, M. C., Yarhouse, M. A., Bucher, E., Leary, A., Sides, J., Silander, N., Statesir, L., & Marin, A. (2014, April). *Christian parents of sexual minority youths speak about helpful resources* [Poster presentation]. Christian Association for Psychological Studies International Conference, Atlanta.

Zaporozhets, O., Sides, J., Yarhouse, M. A., Myers, K., Campbell, M., Lane, C., Baker, C., Leary, A., Houp, D., Ajex, J., Trotta, K., Hamling, C., Statesir, L., & Marin, A. (2015, March). "What do you mean you are gay?" Messages that Christian parents hear when LGBT youth are coming out (Preliminary results based on 150 cases) [Presentation]. Christian Association for Psychological Studies National Conference, Pasadena, California.

INDEX

ALSO AVAILABLE

Understanding Gender Dysphoria
Mark A. Yarhouse
978-0-8308-2859-3

Gender Identity & Faith
Mark A. Yarhouse & Julia A. Sadusky
978-0-8308-4181-3

Family Therapies
Mark A. Yarhouse and James N. Sells
978-0-8308-2854-8